Dedicated to my family, and all the Ladies that have influenced my life.

This collection of drawings represents 31 days of drawing positive images of black women in October of 2016. This is not a book of pin up girls, but strong women with a sense of style and strength, I hope you enjoy this collection of drawings, I enjoyed doing them!

-Grady Williams III

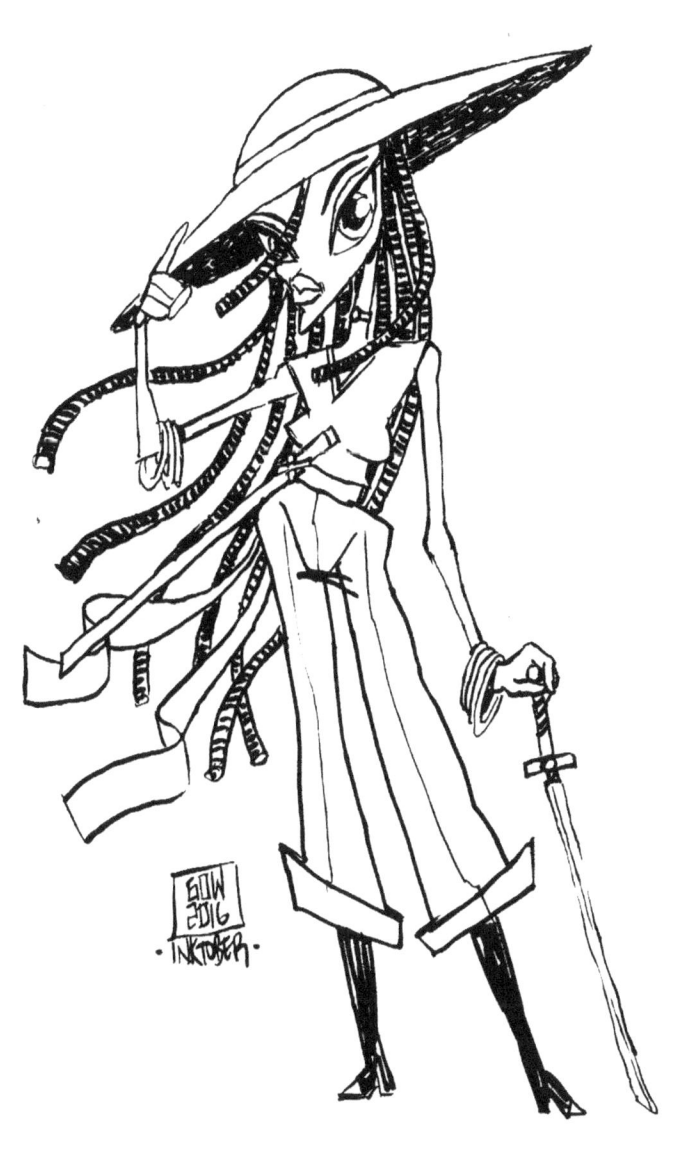

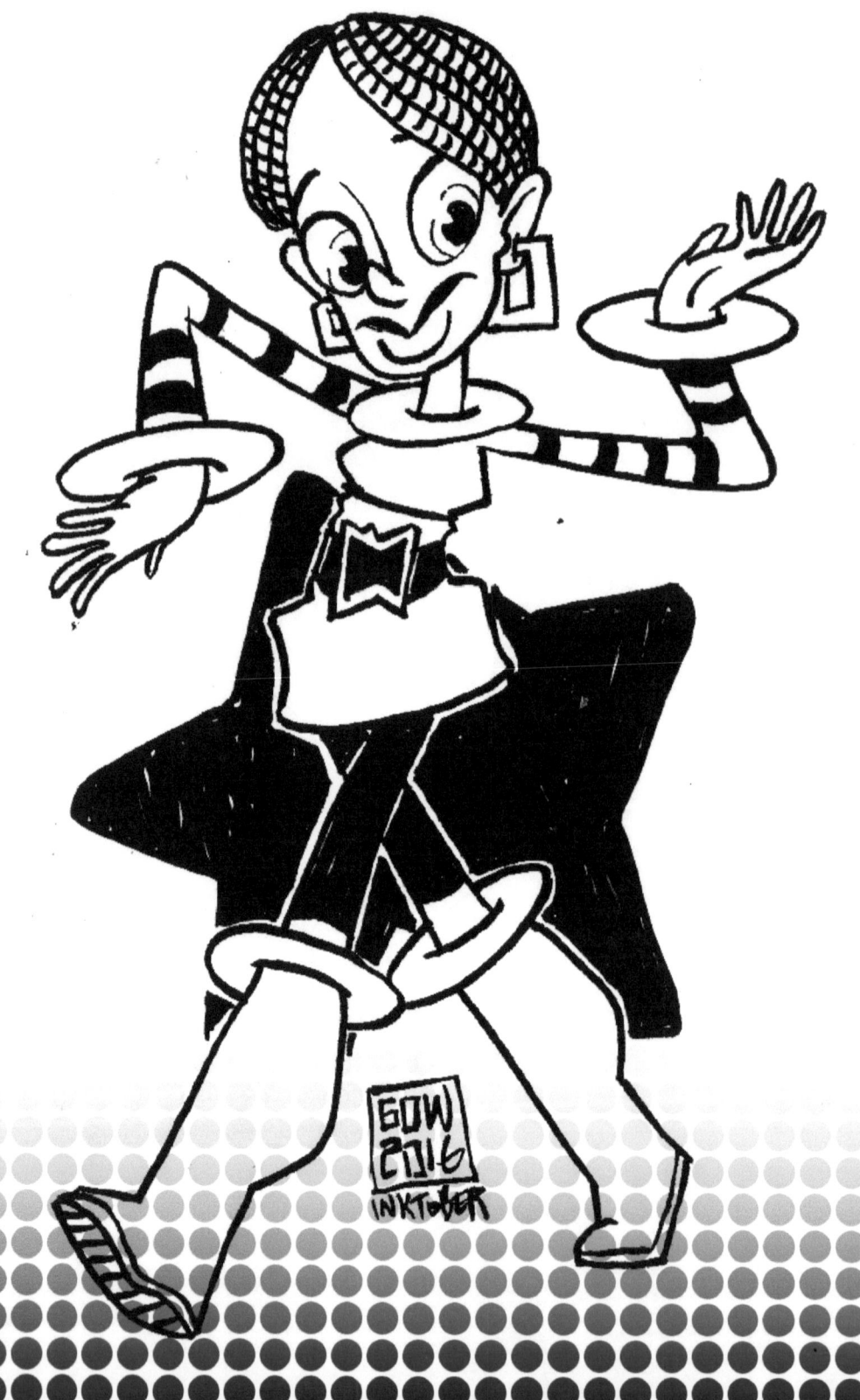

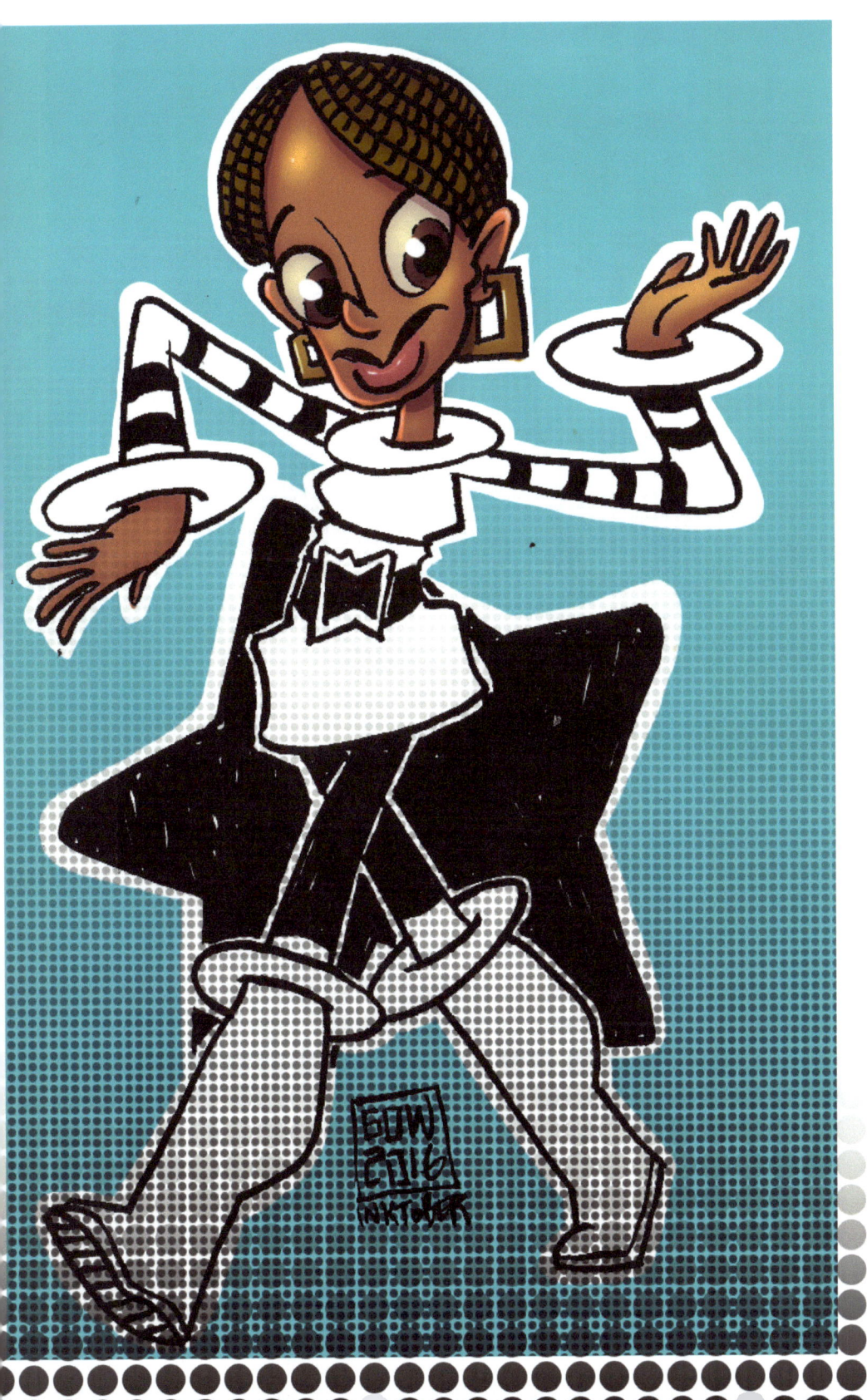

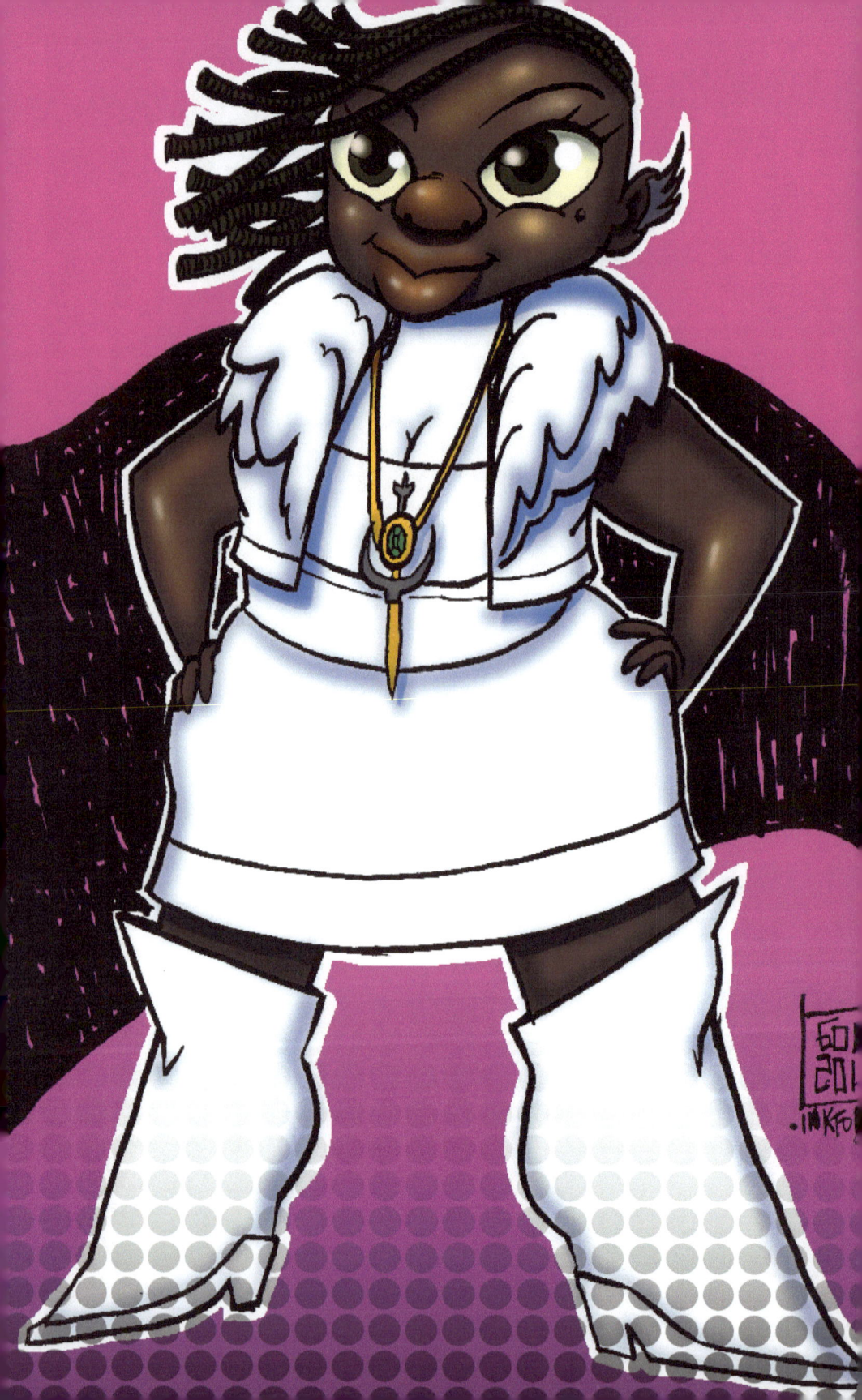

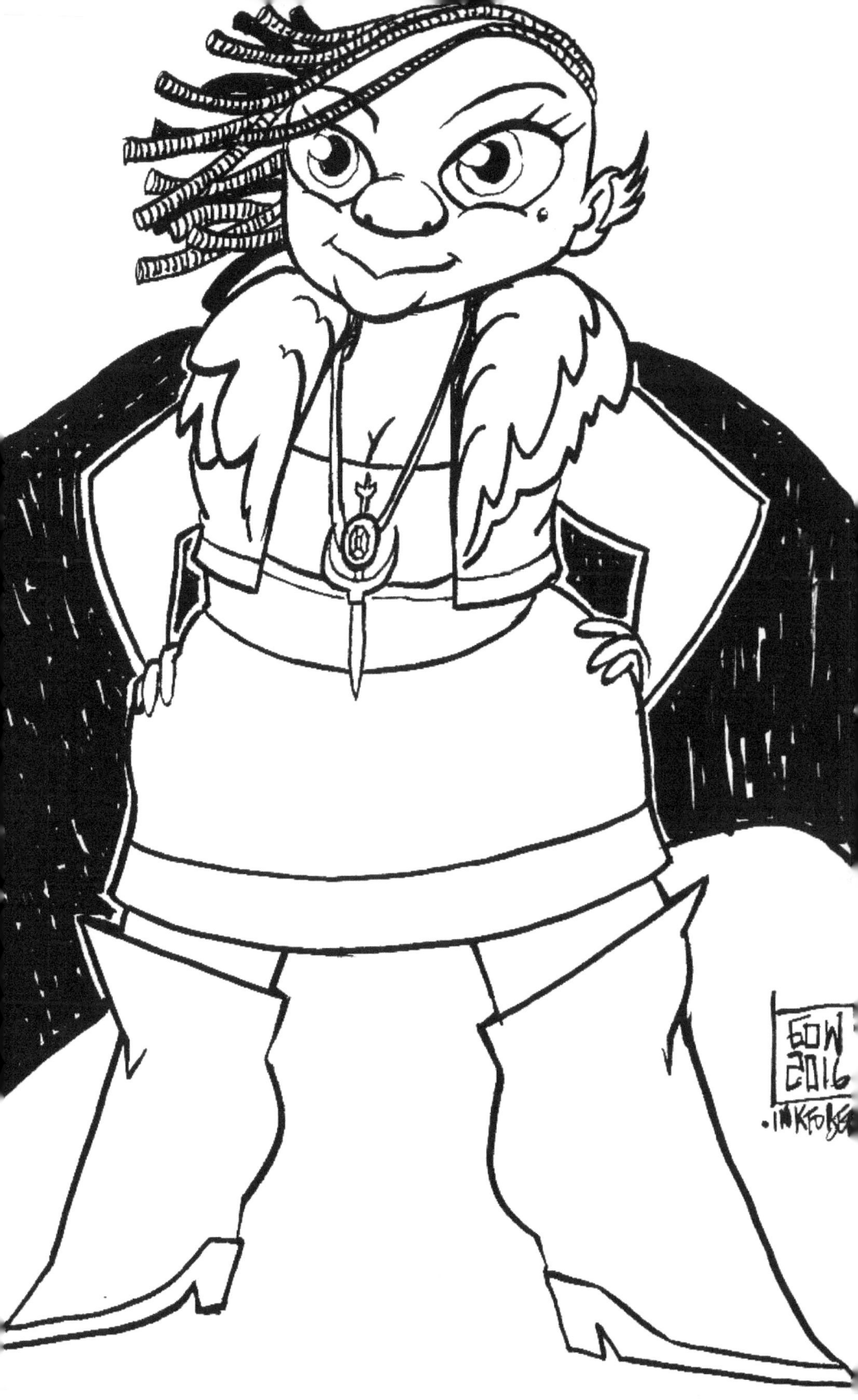

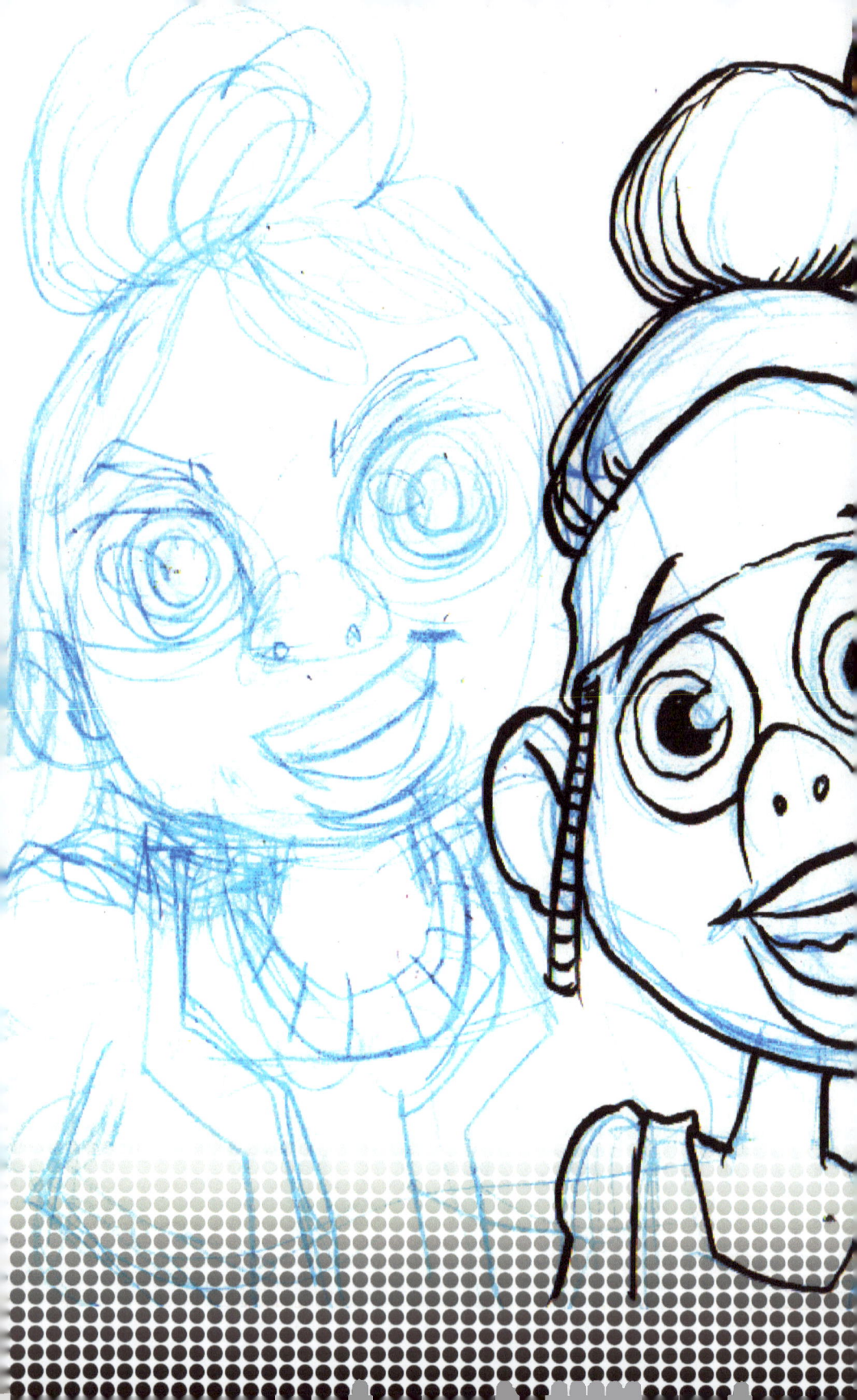

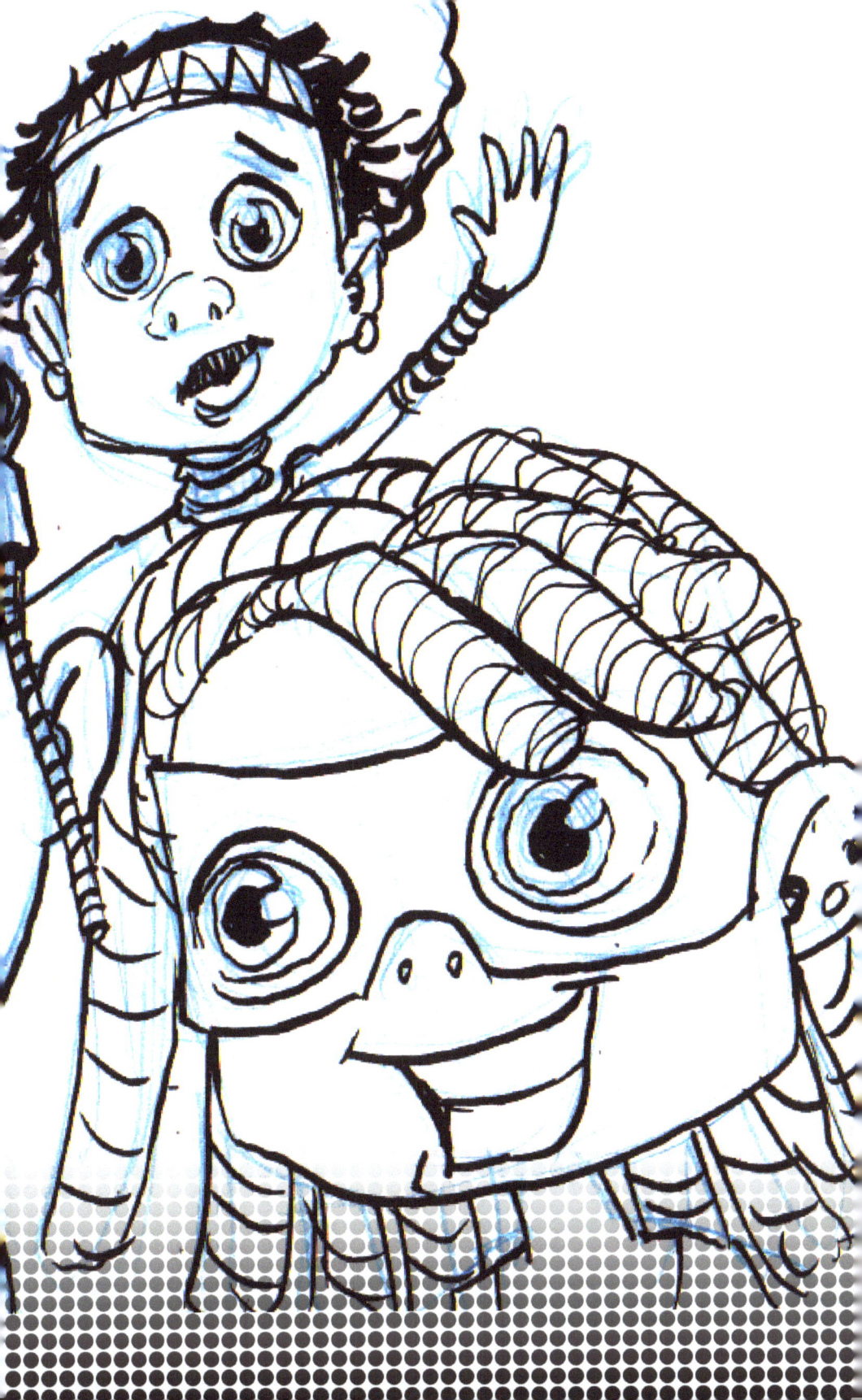

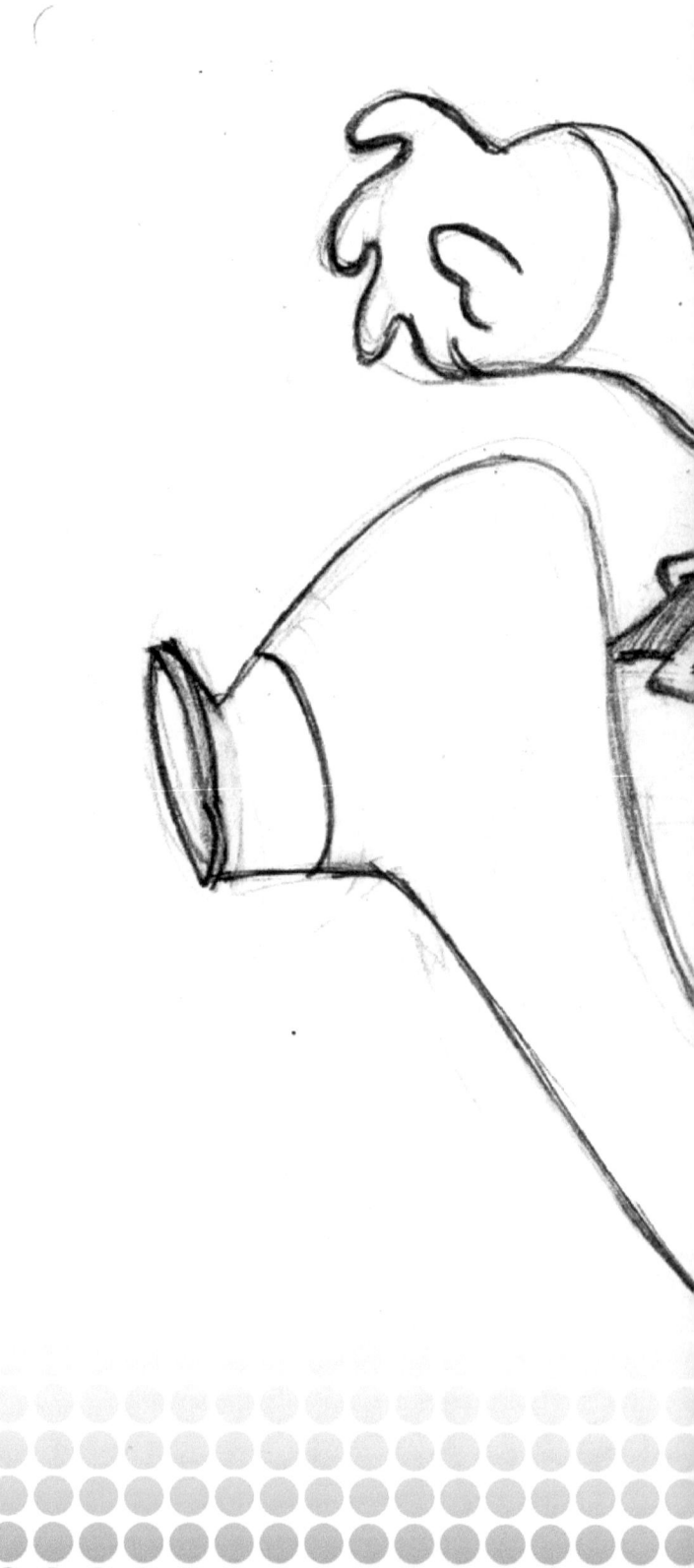

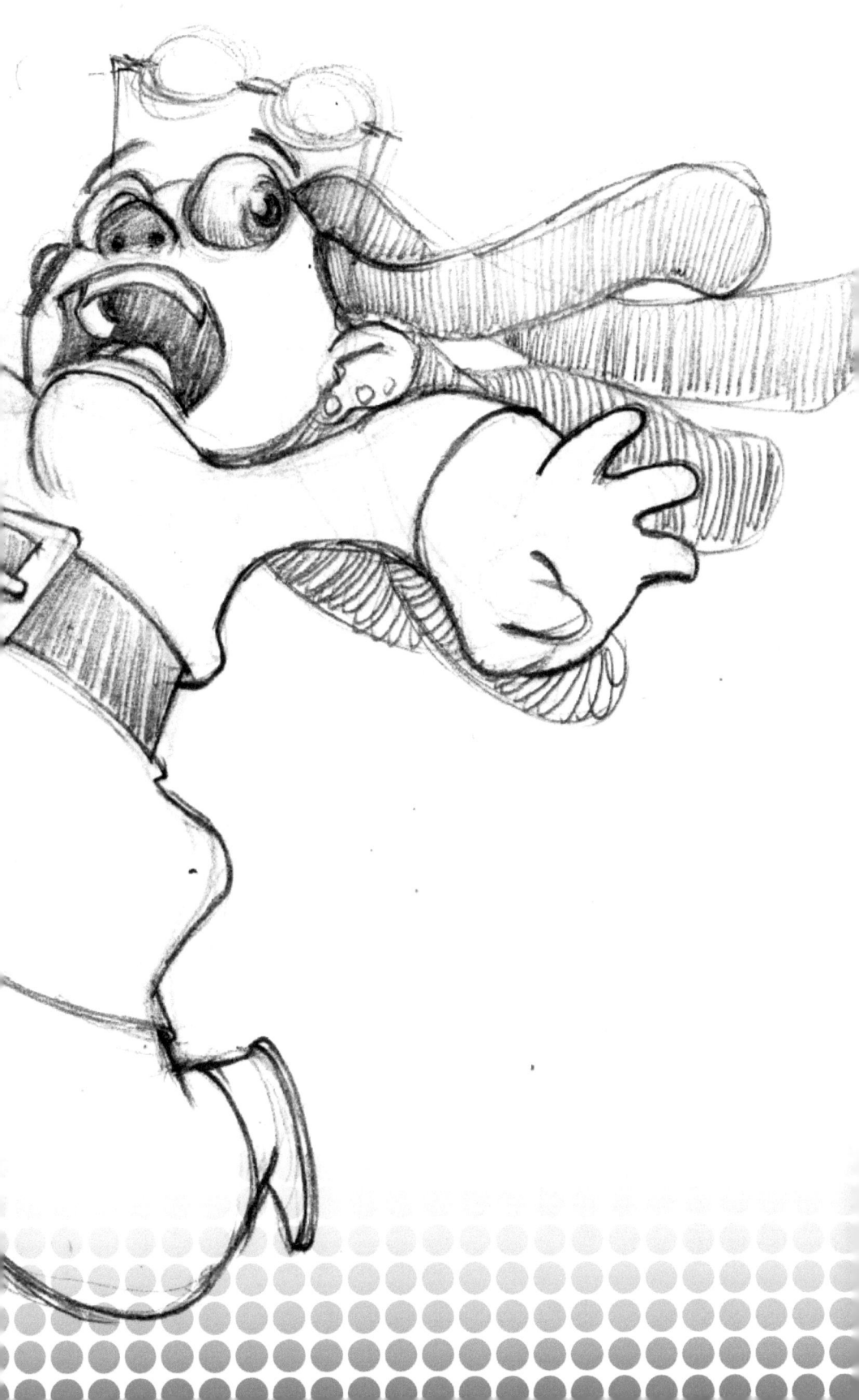

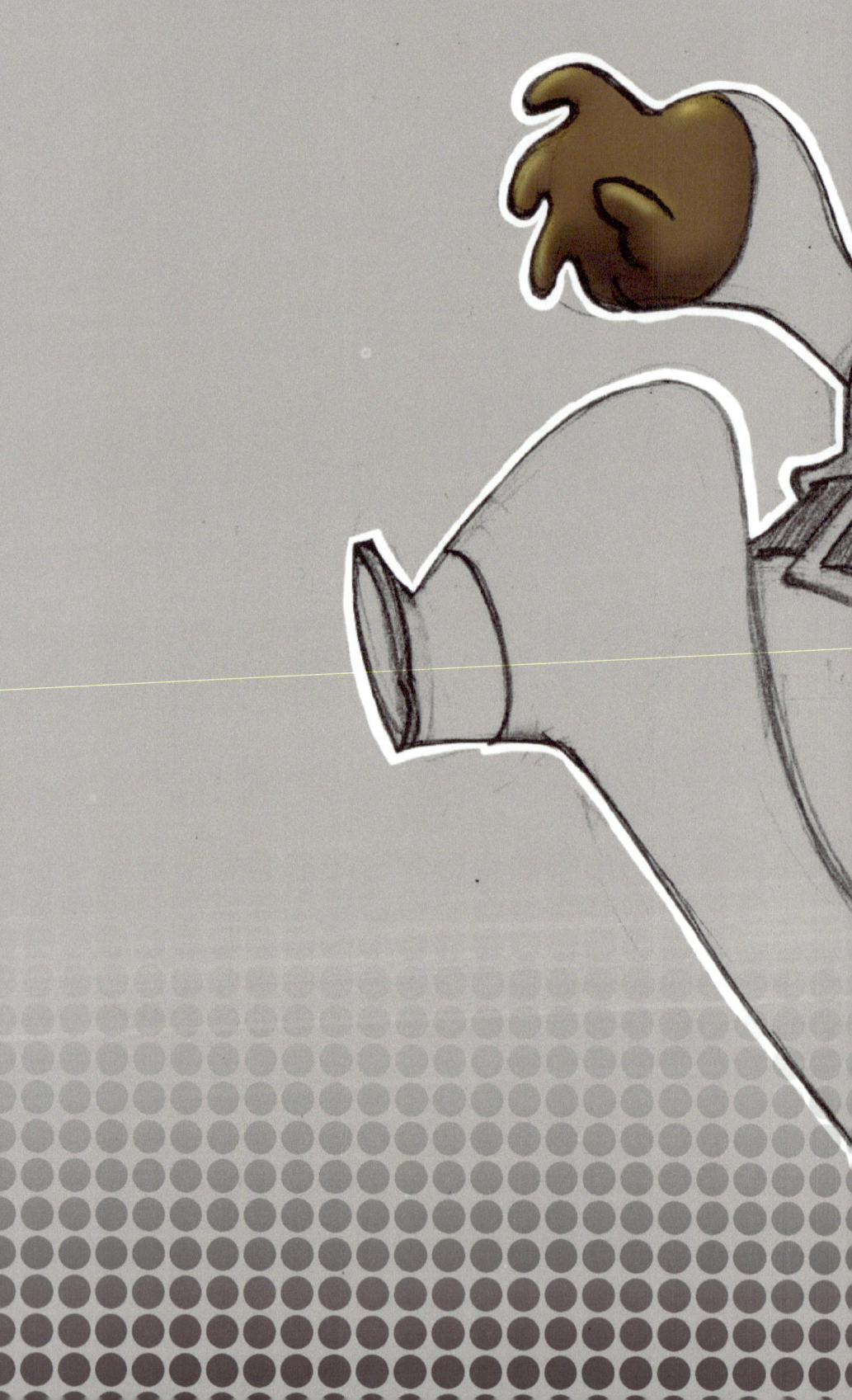

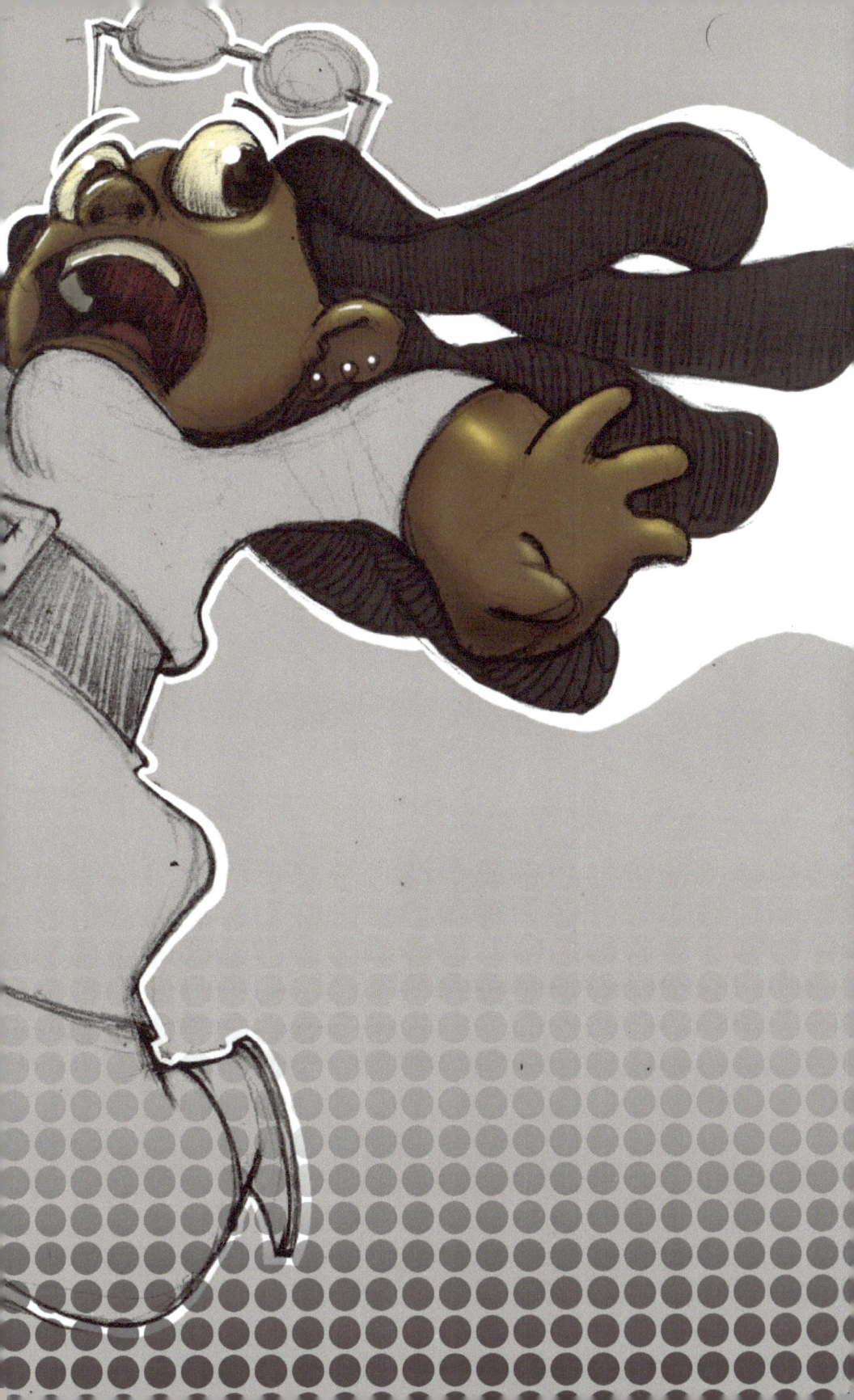

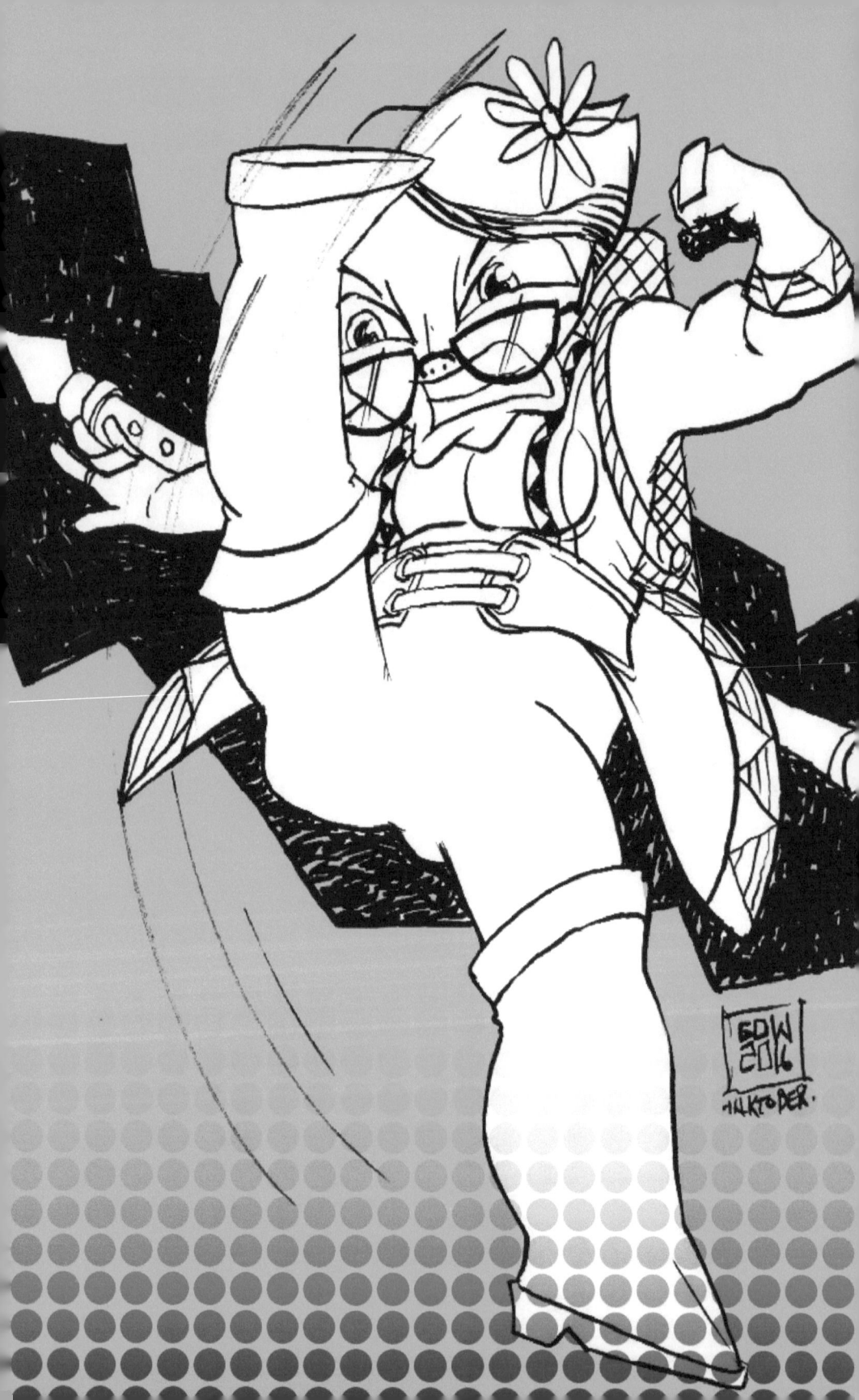

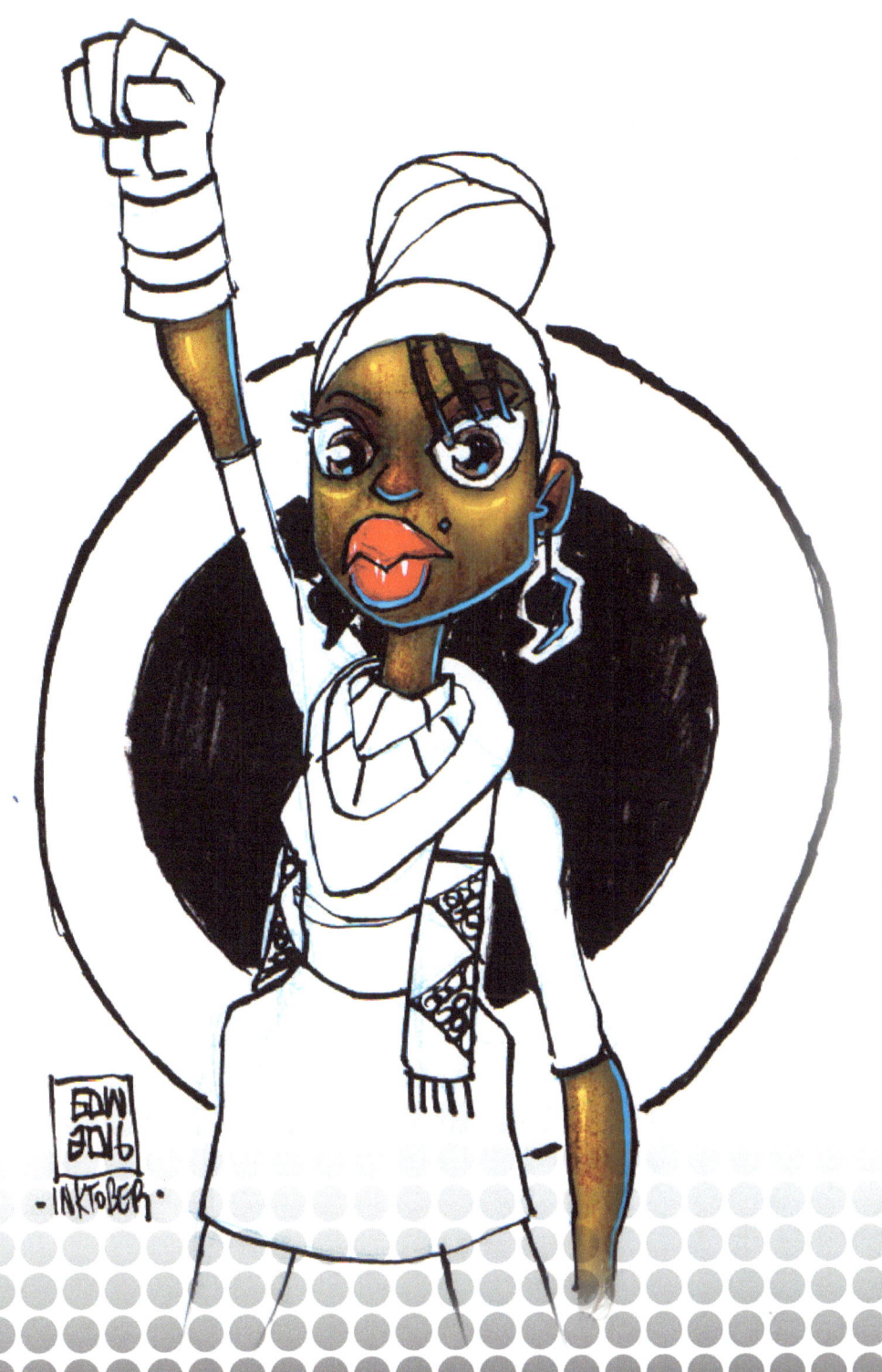

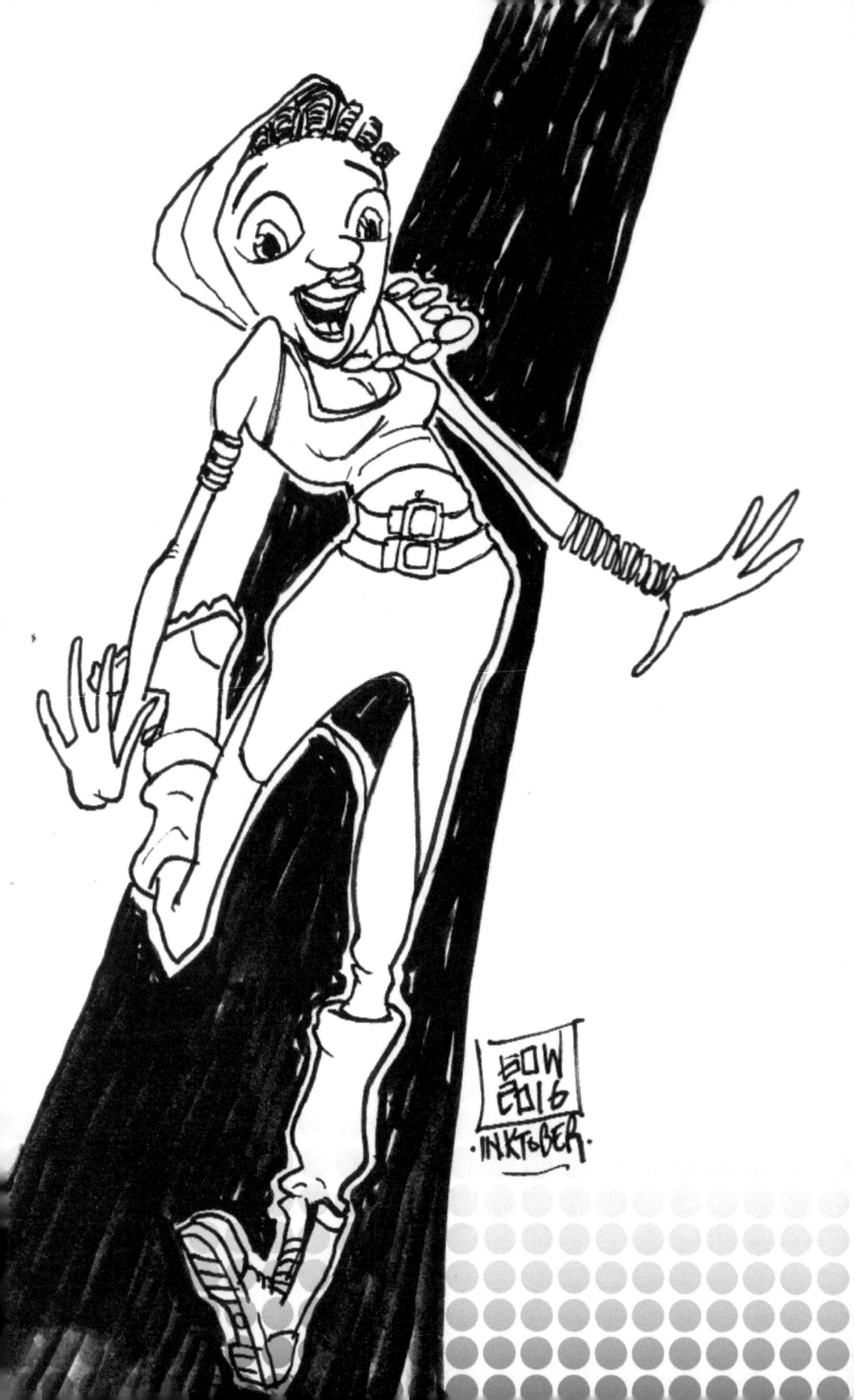

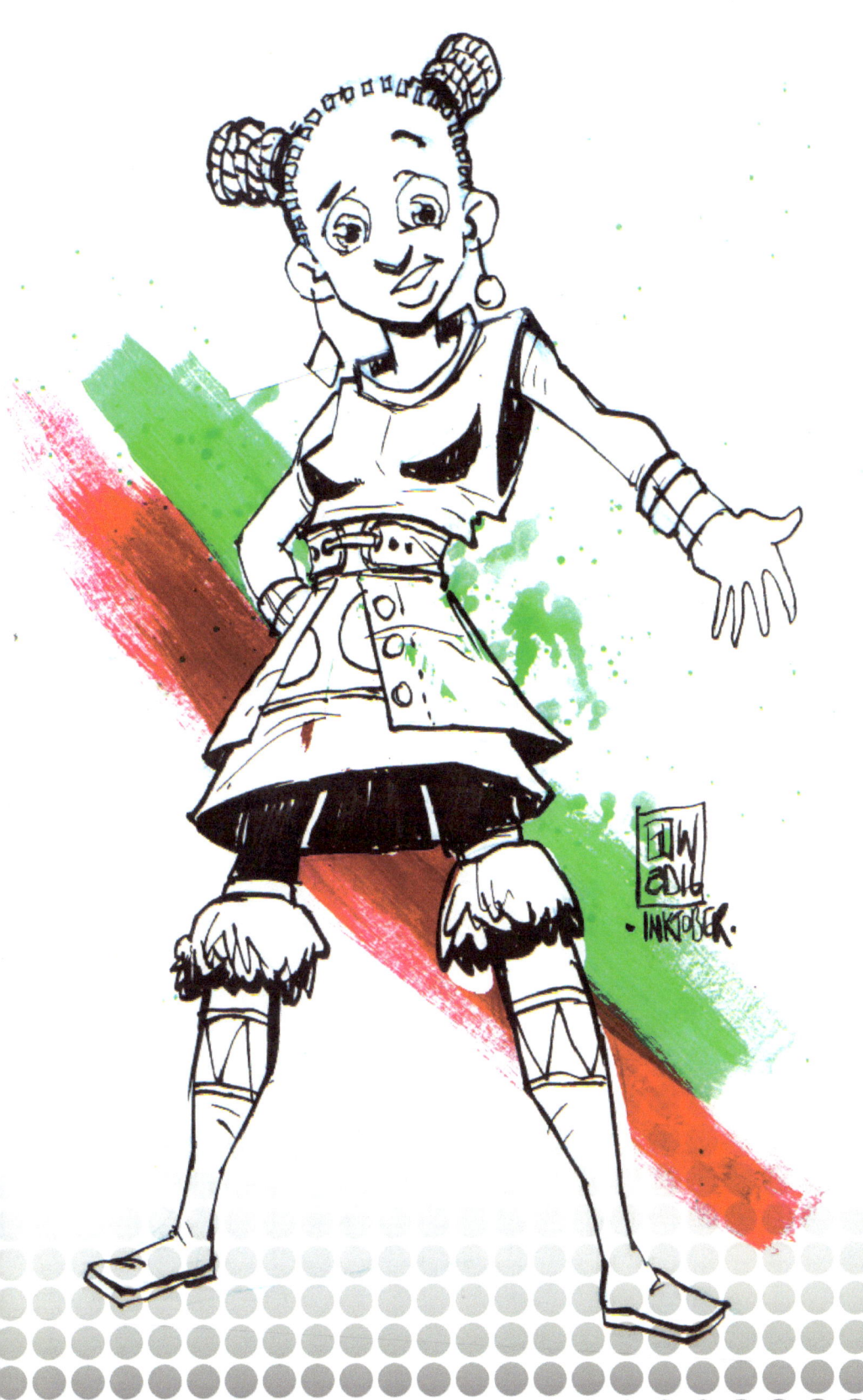

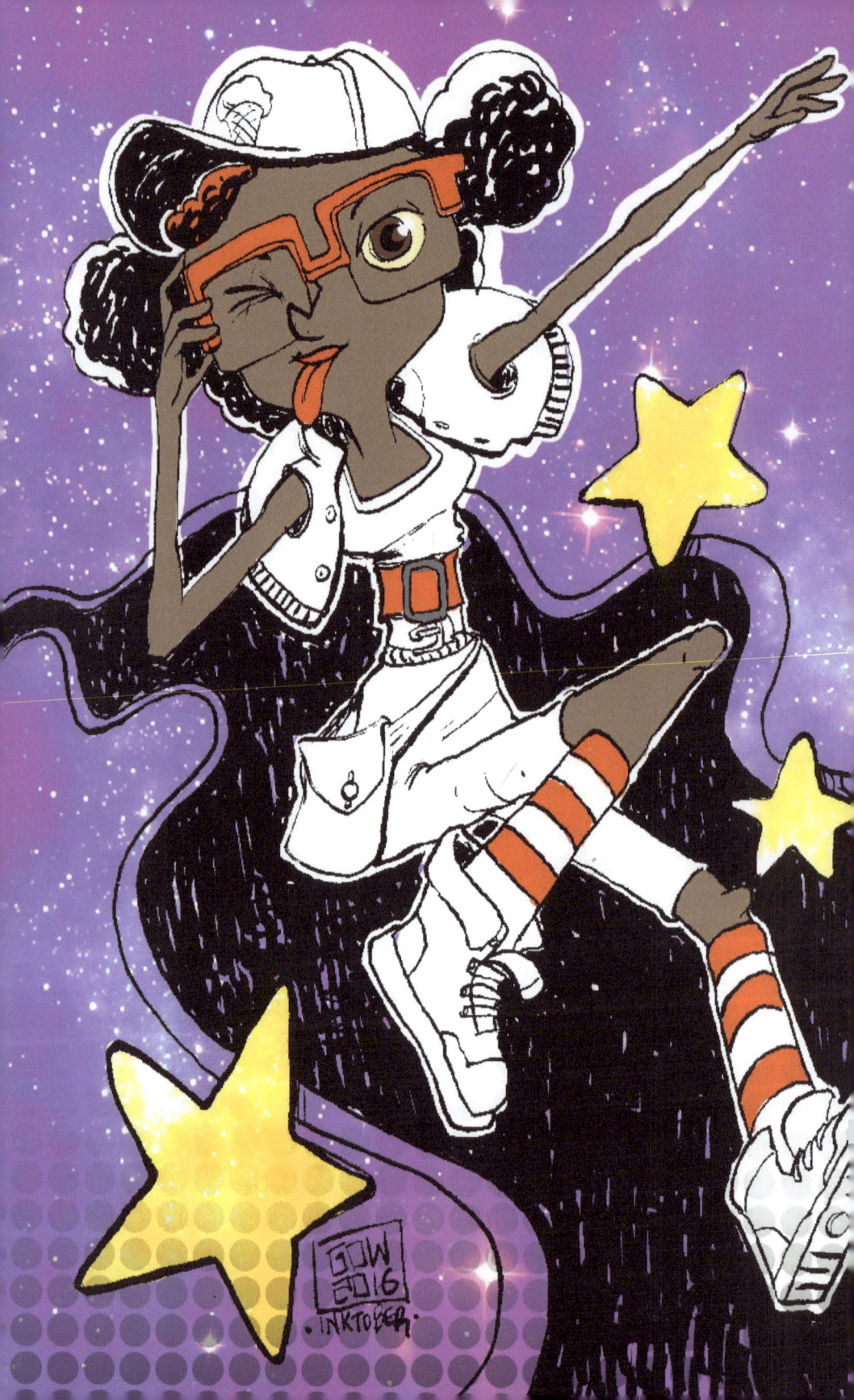

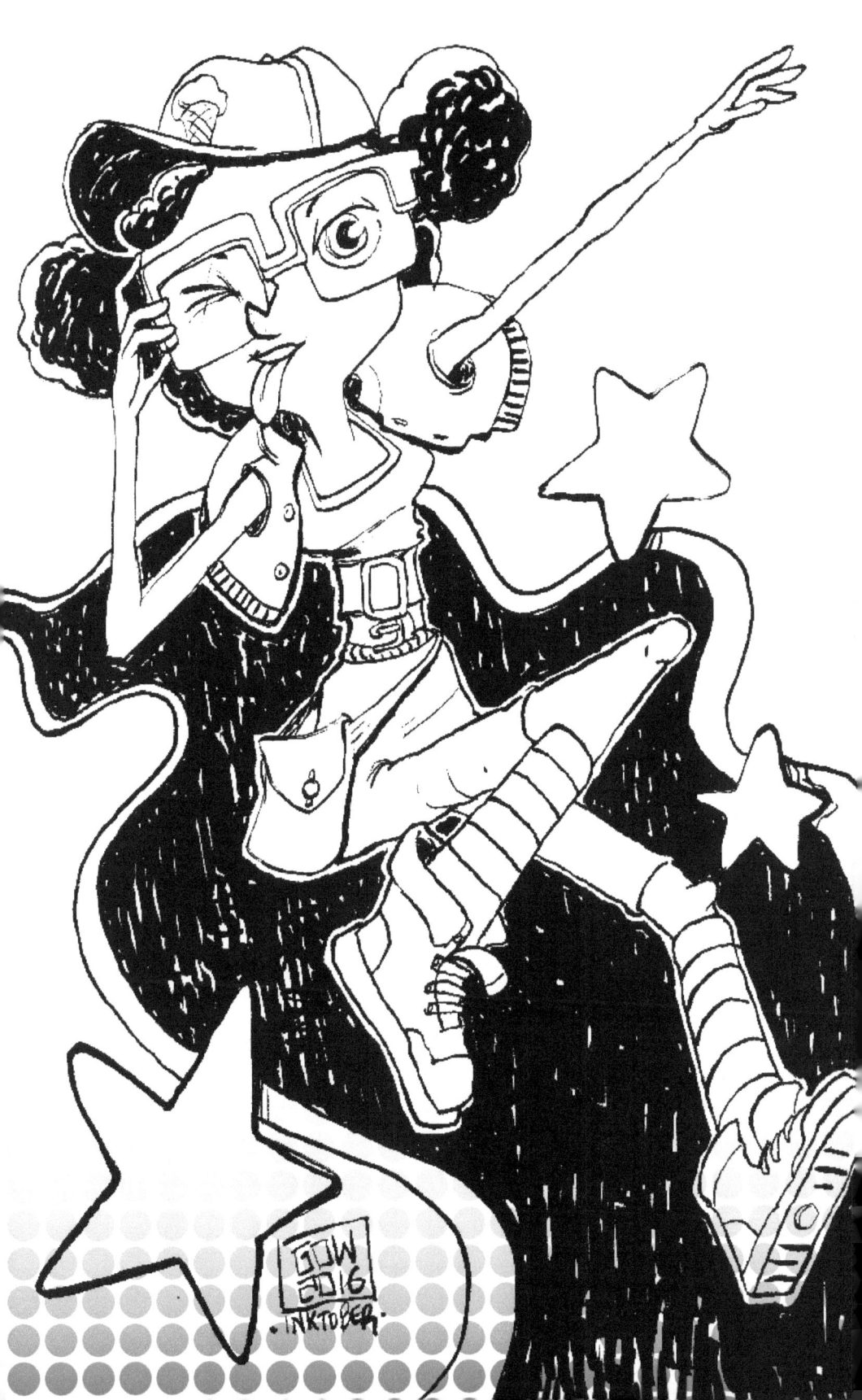

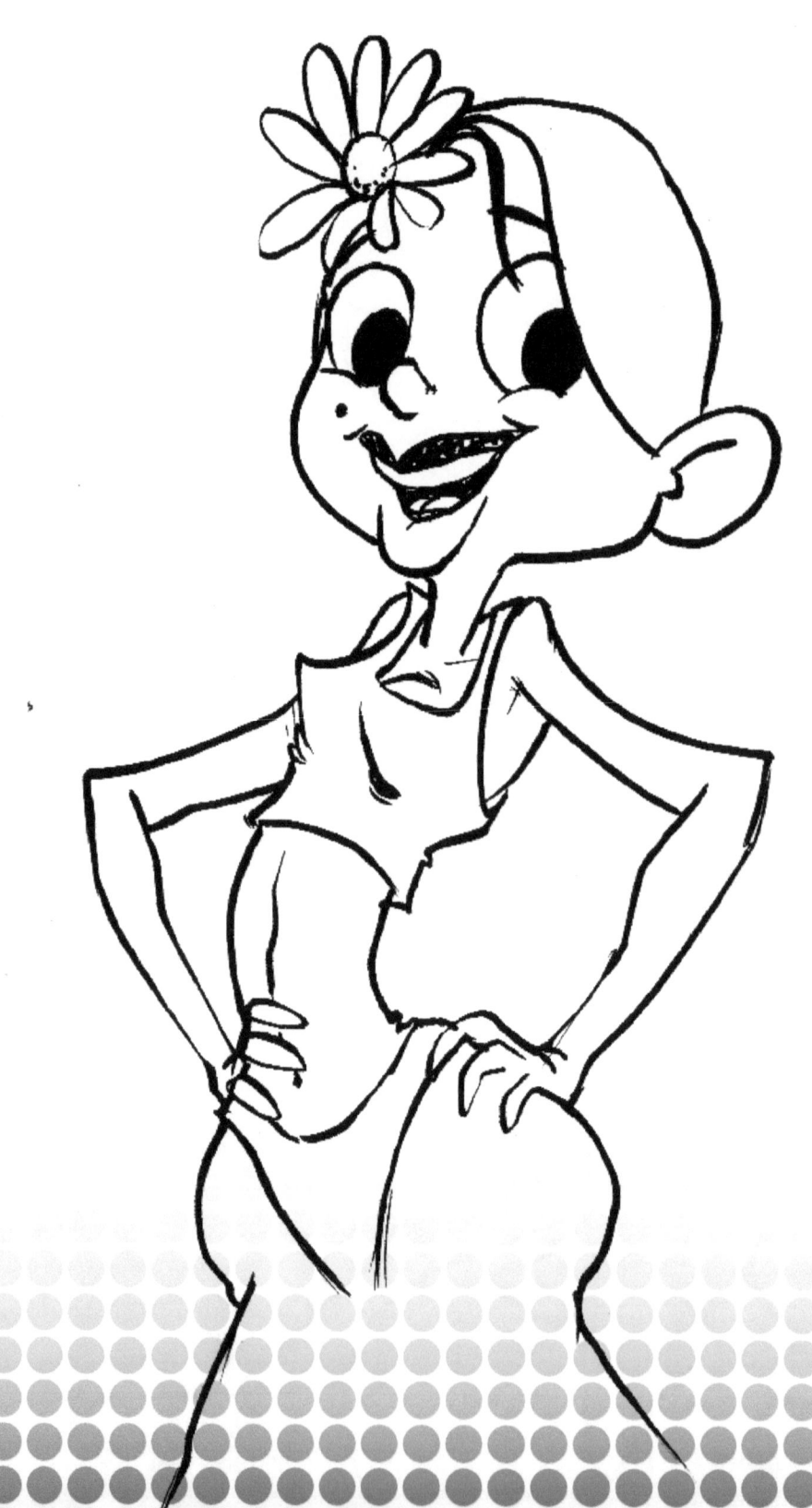

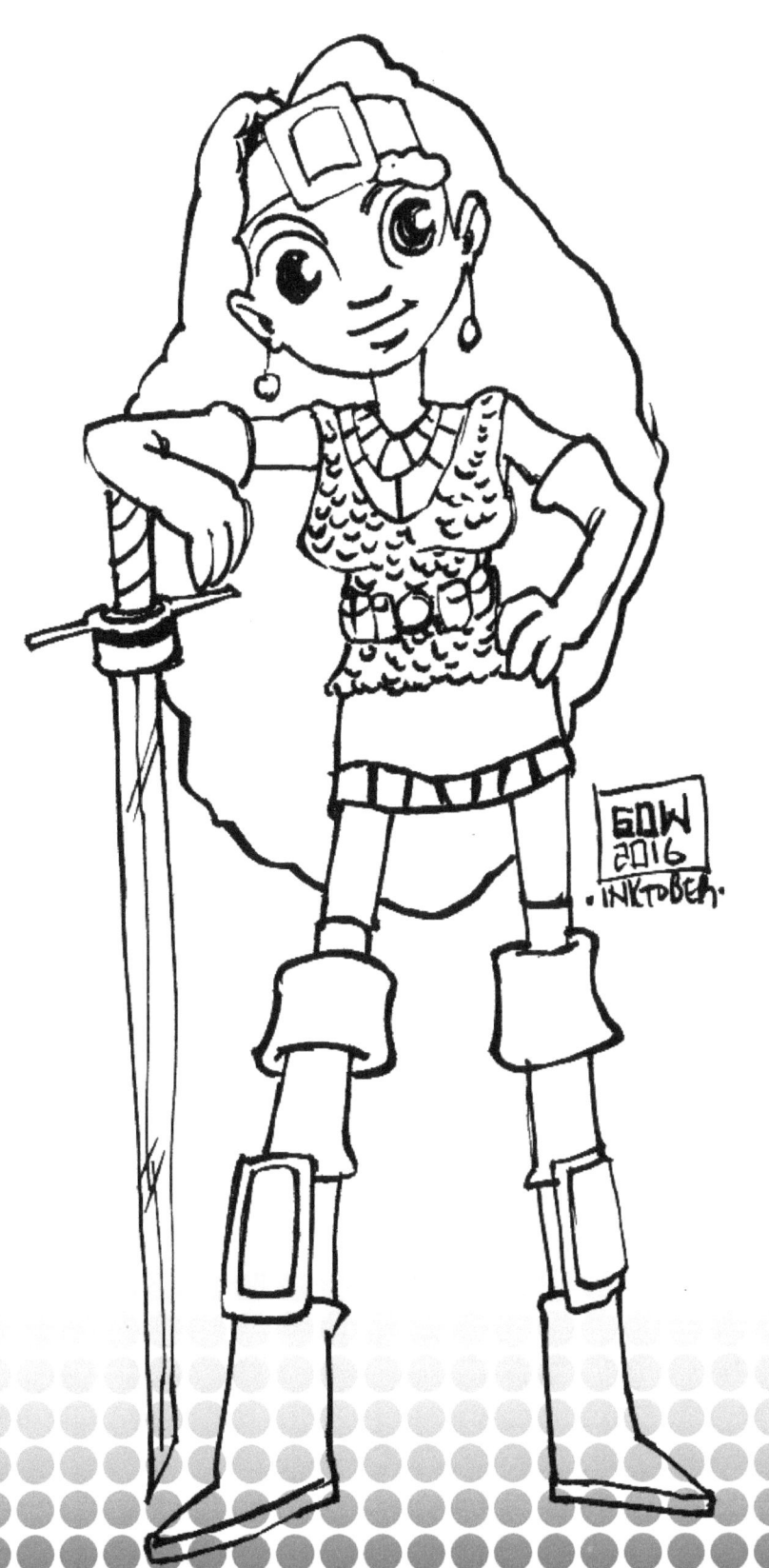

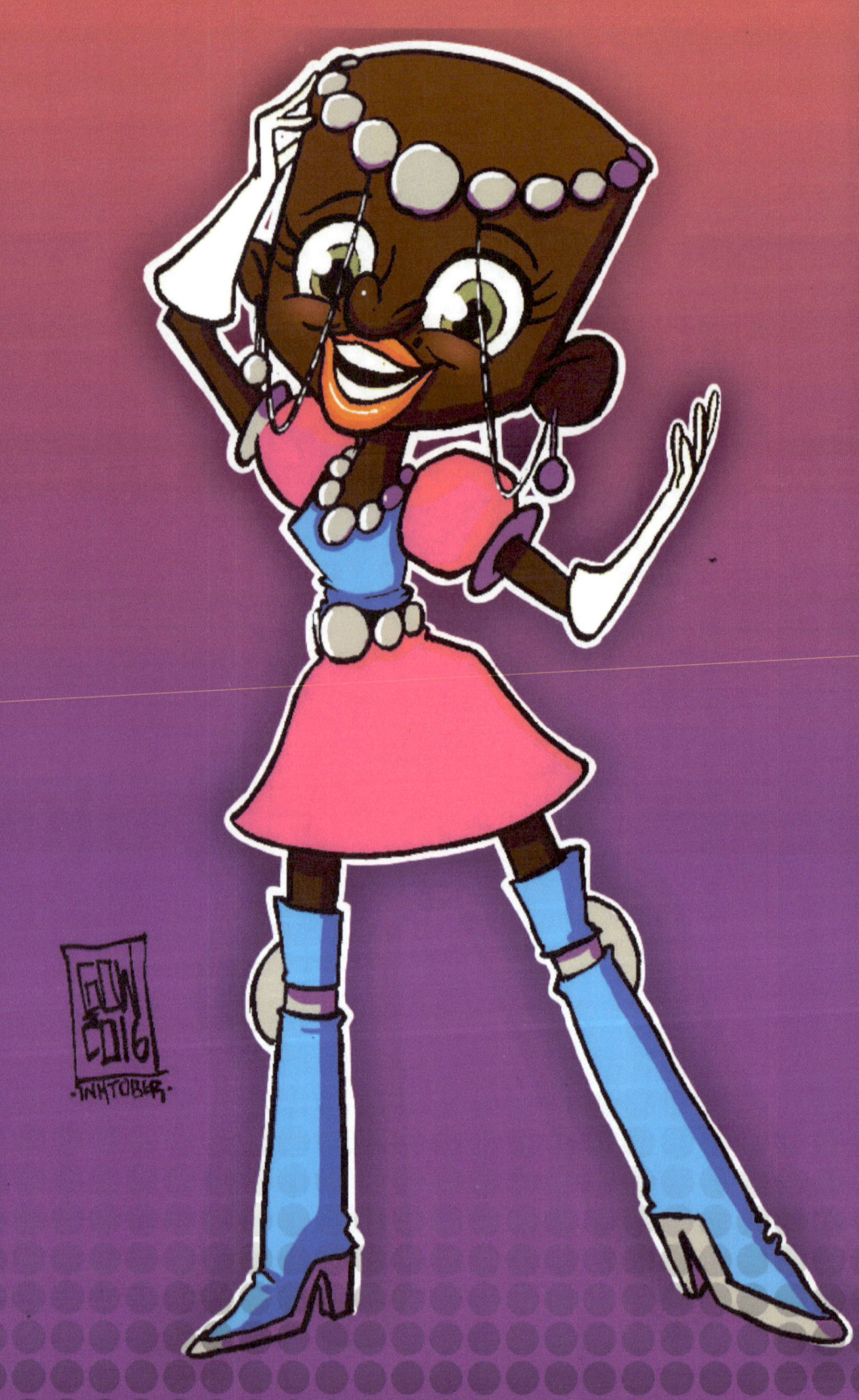

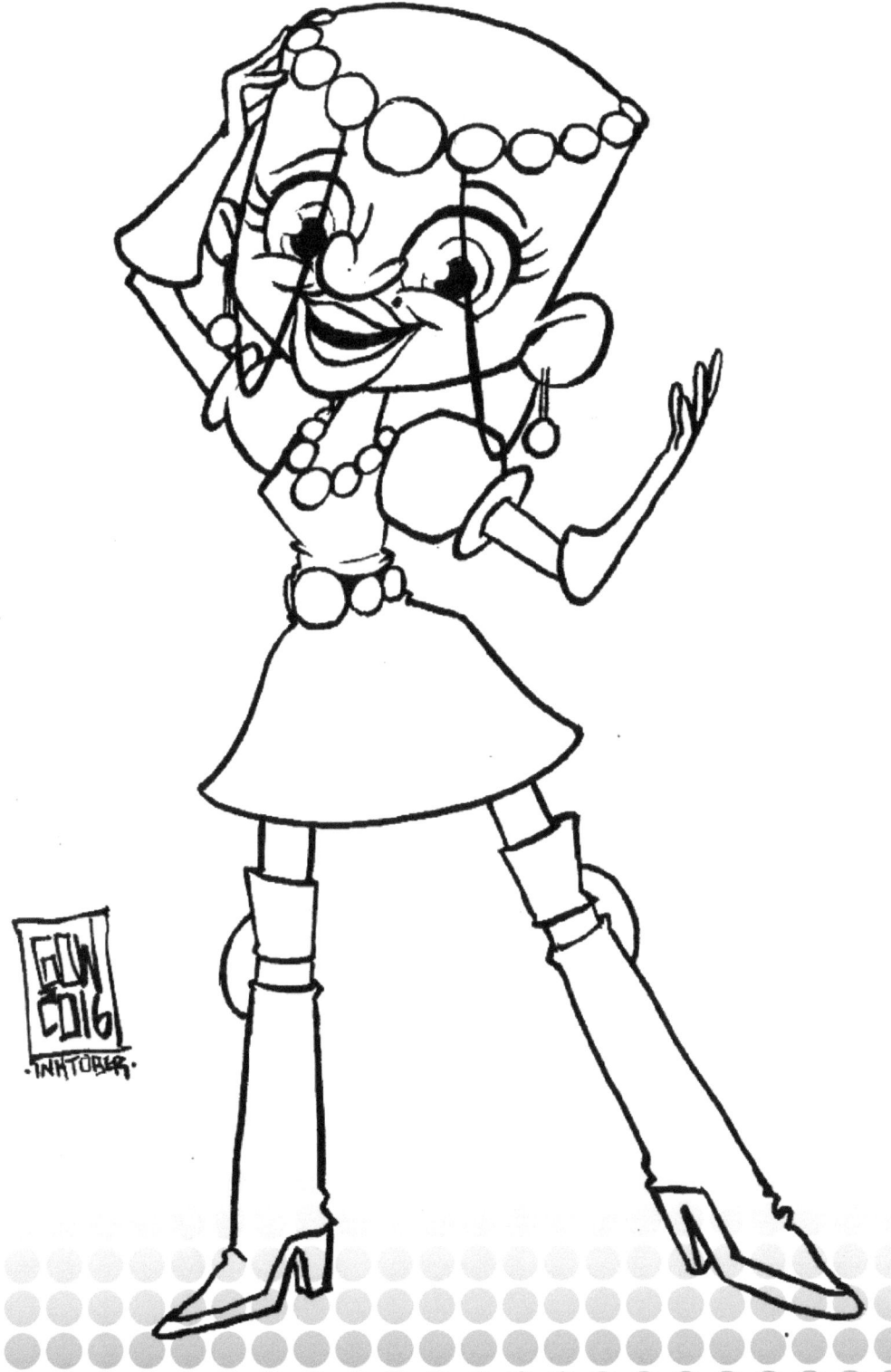

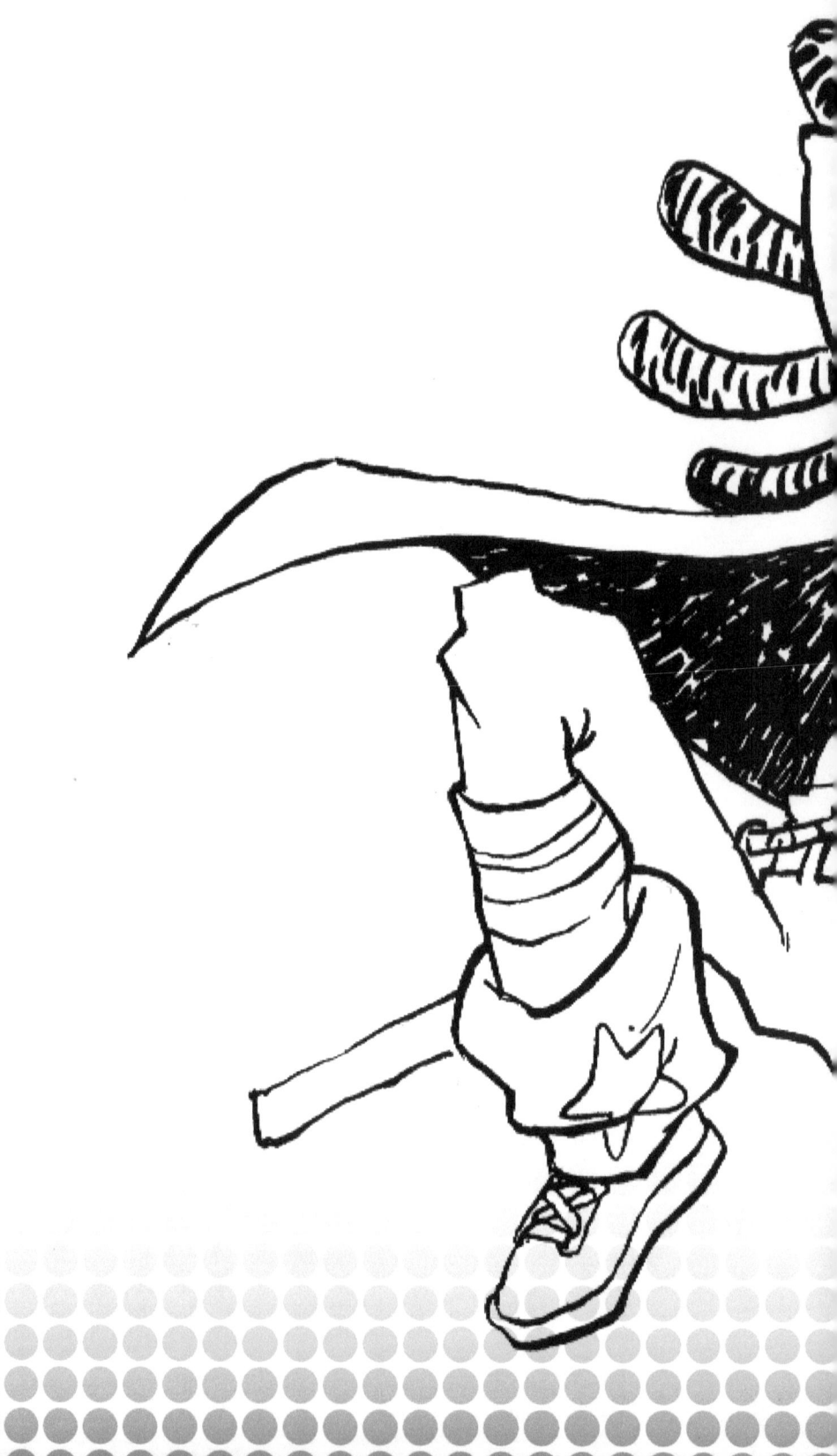

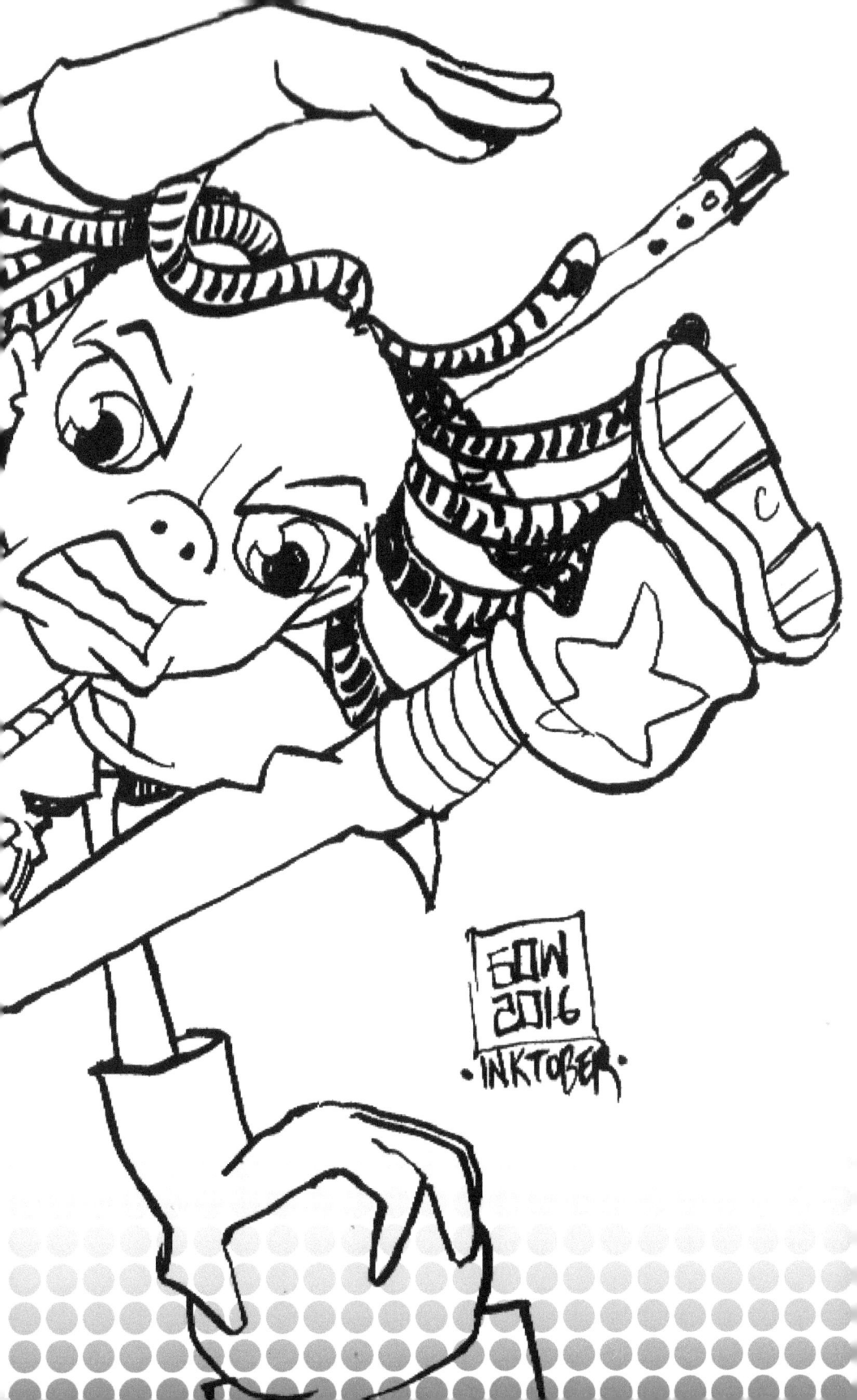

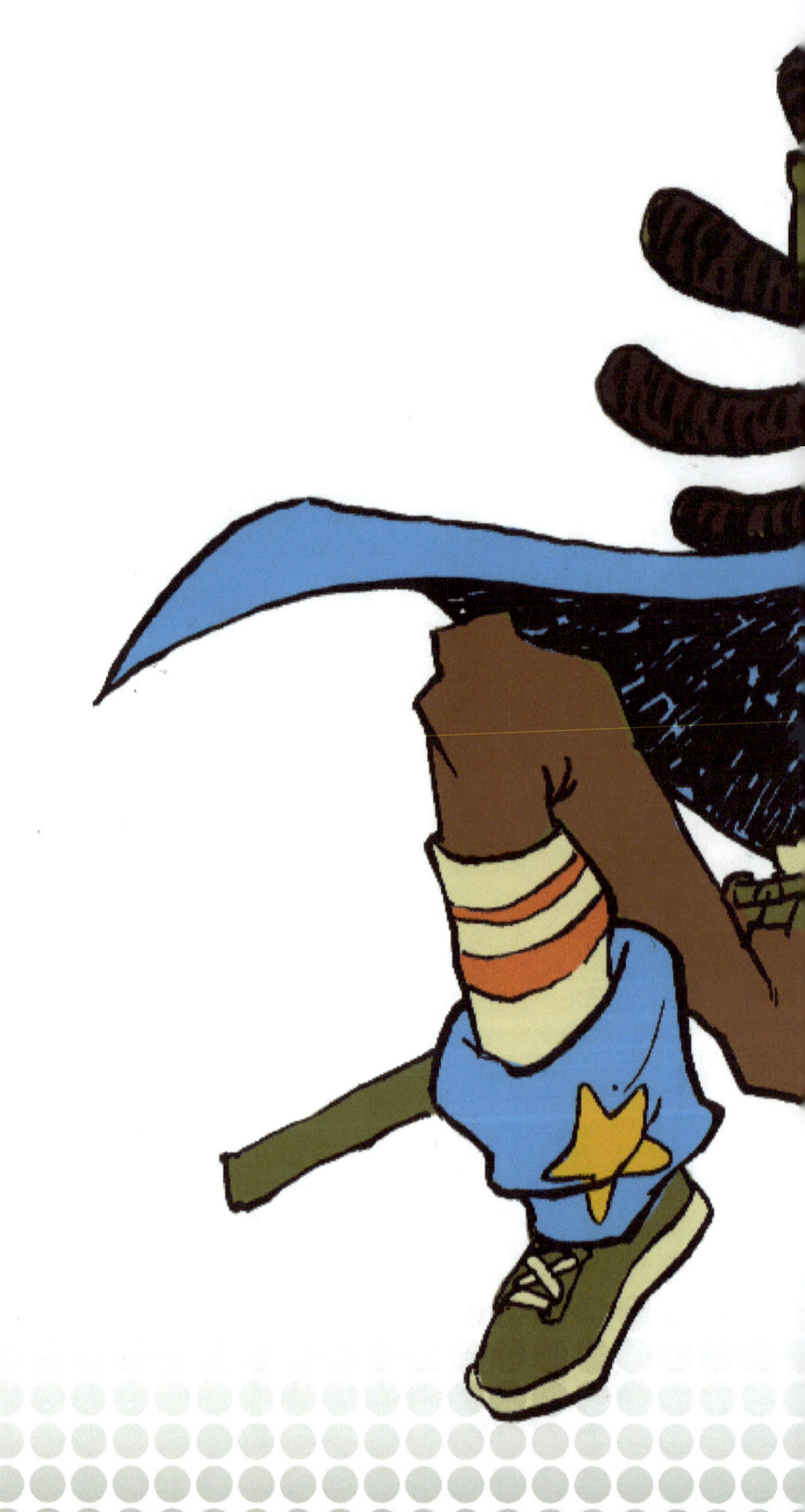

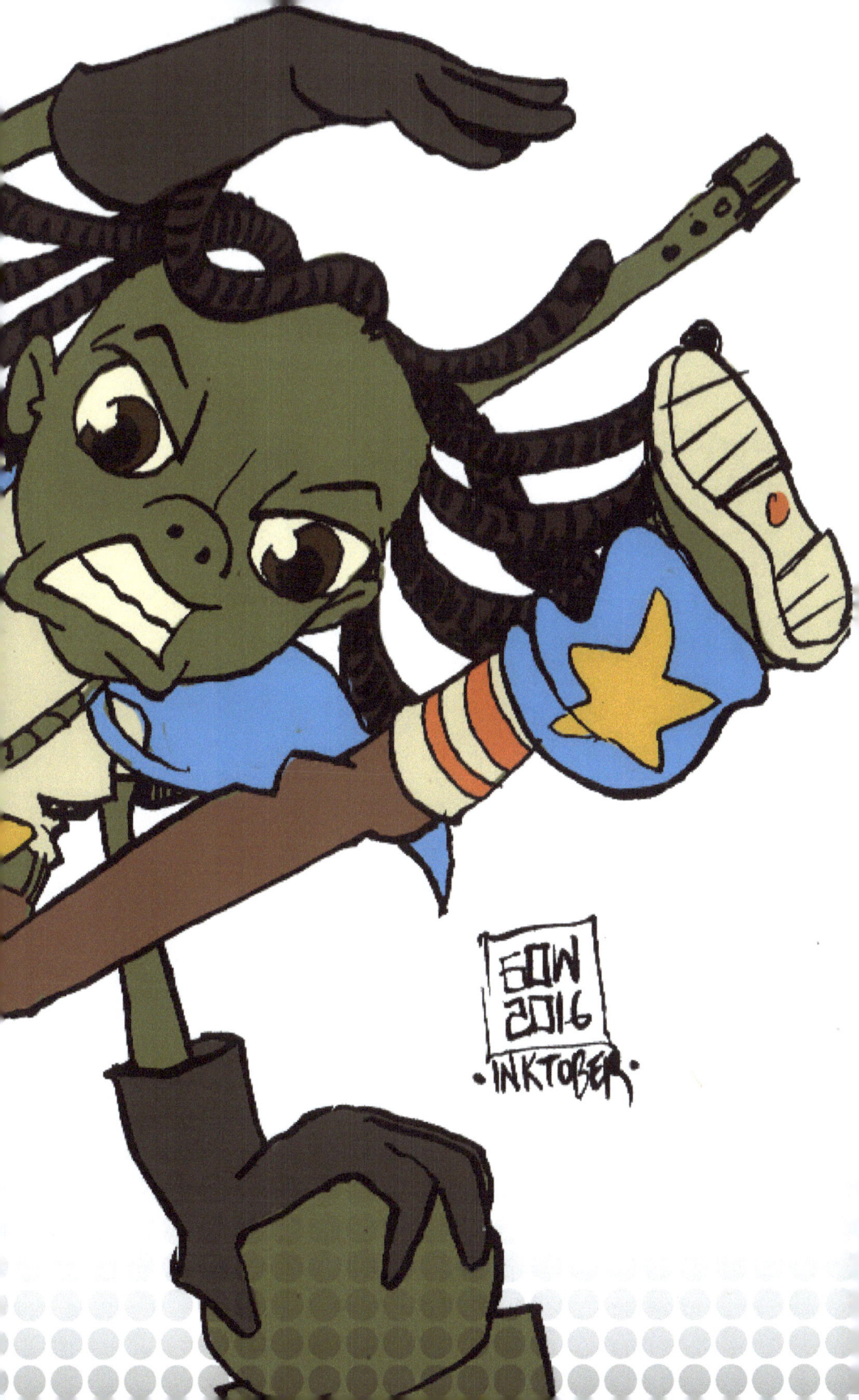

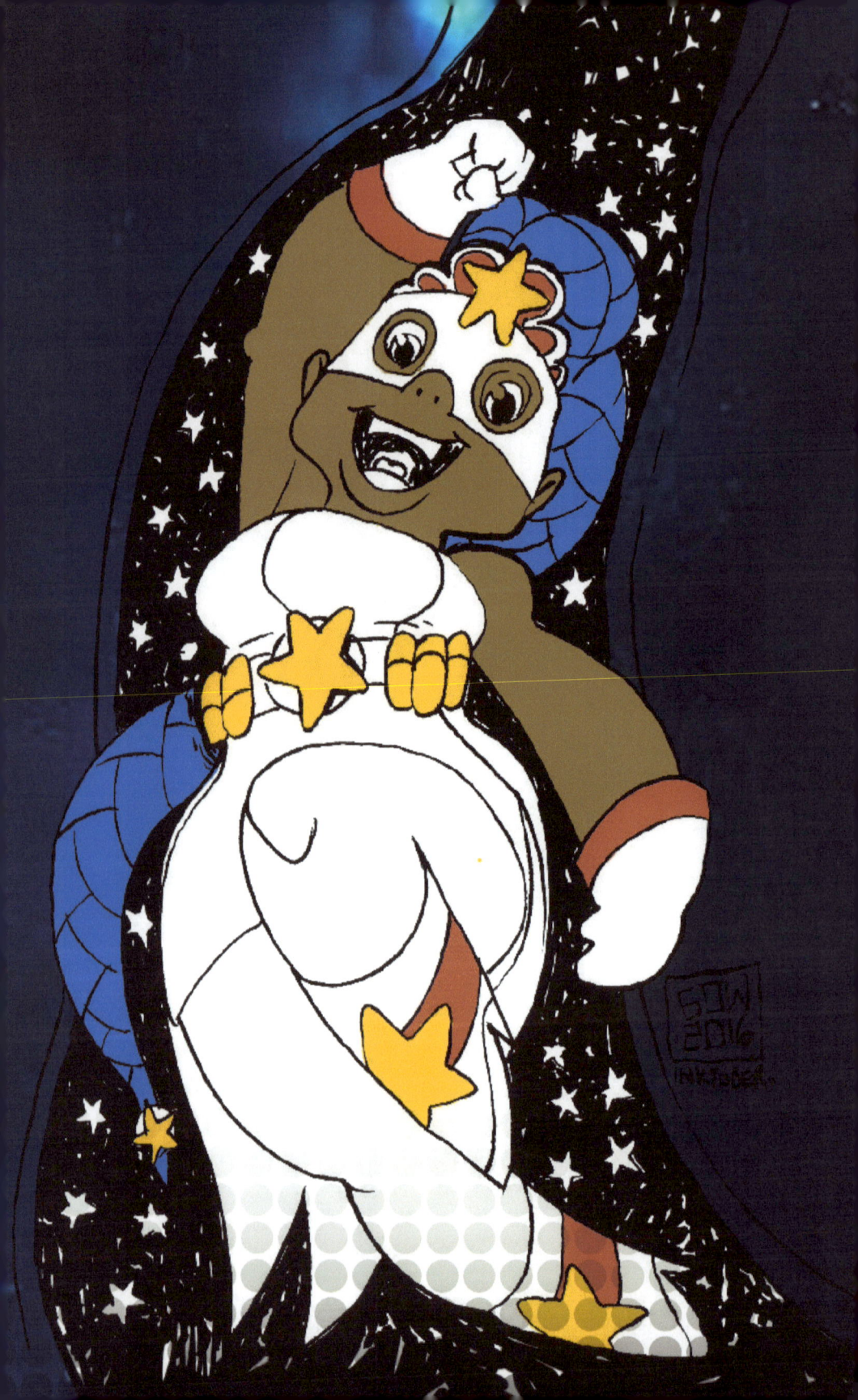

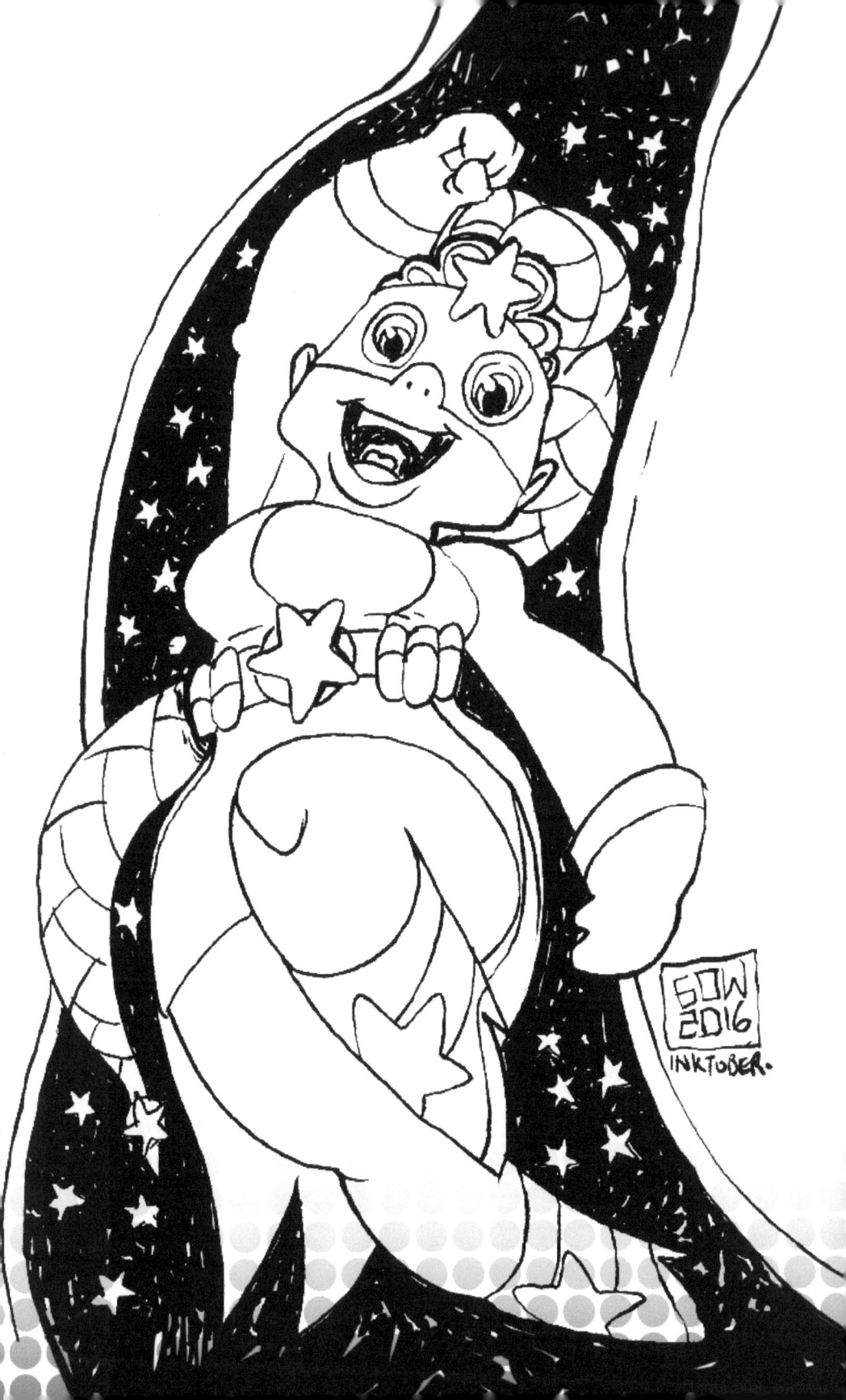

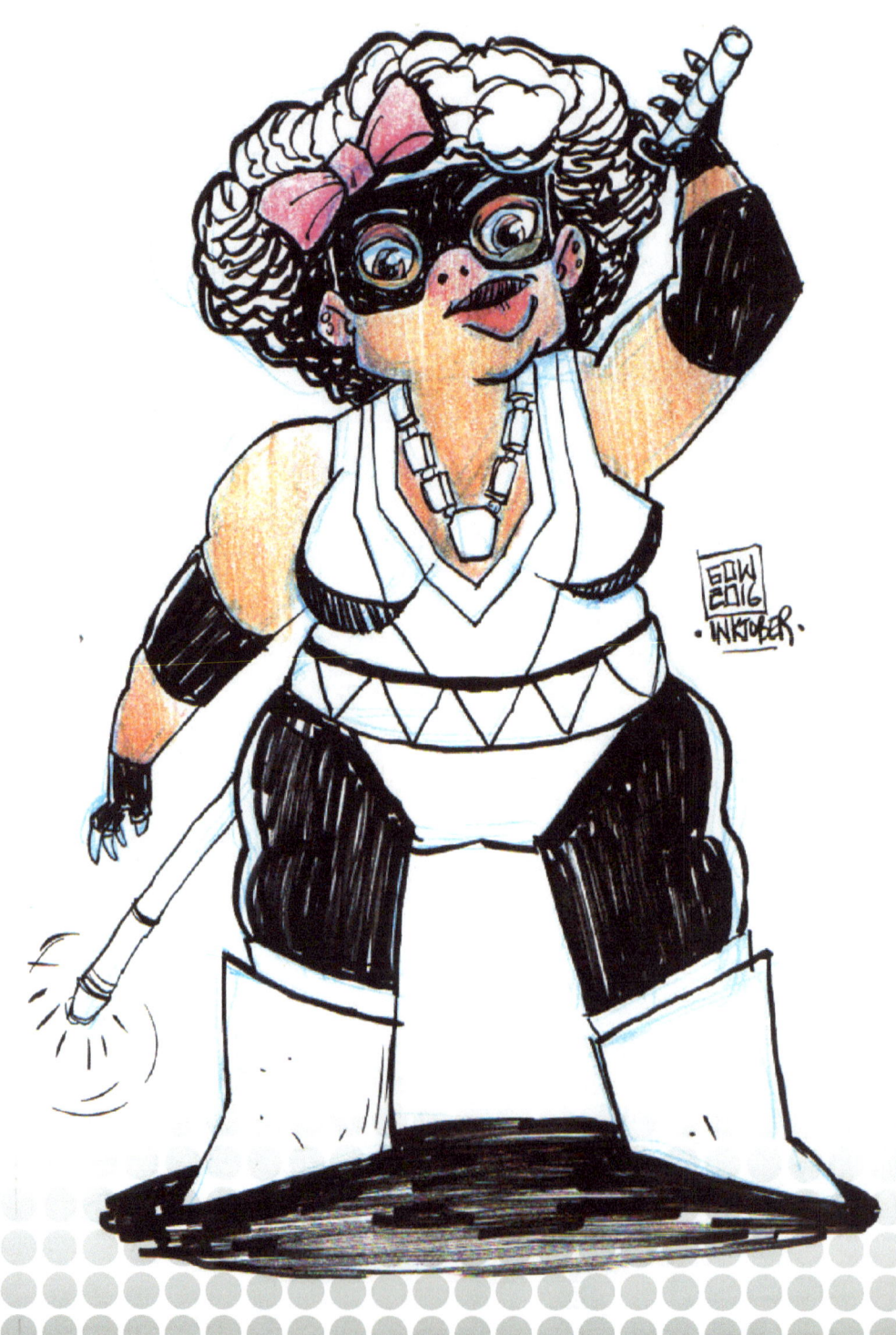

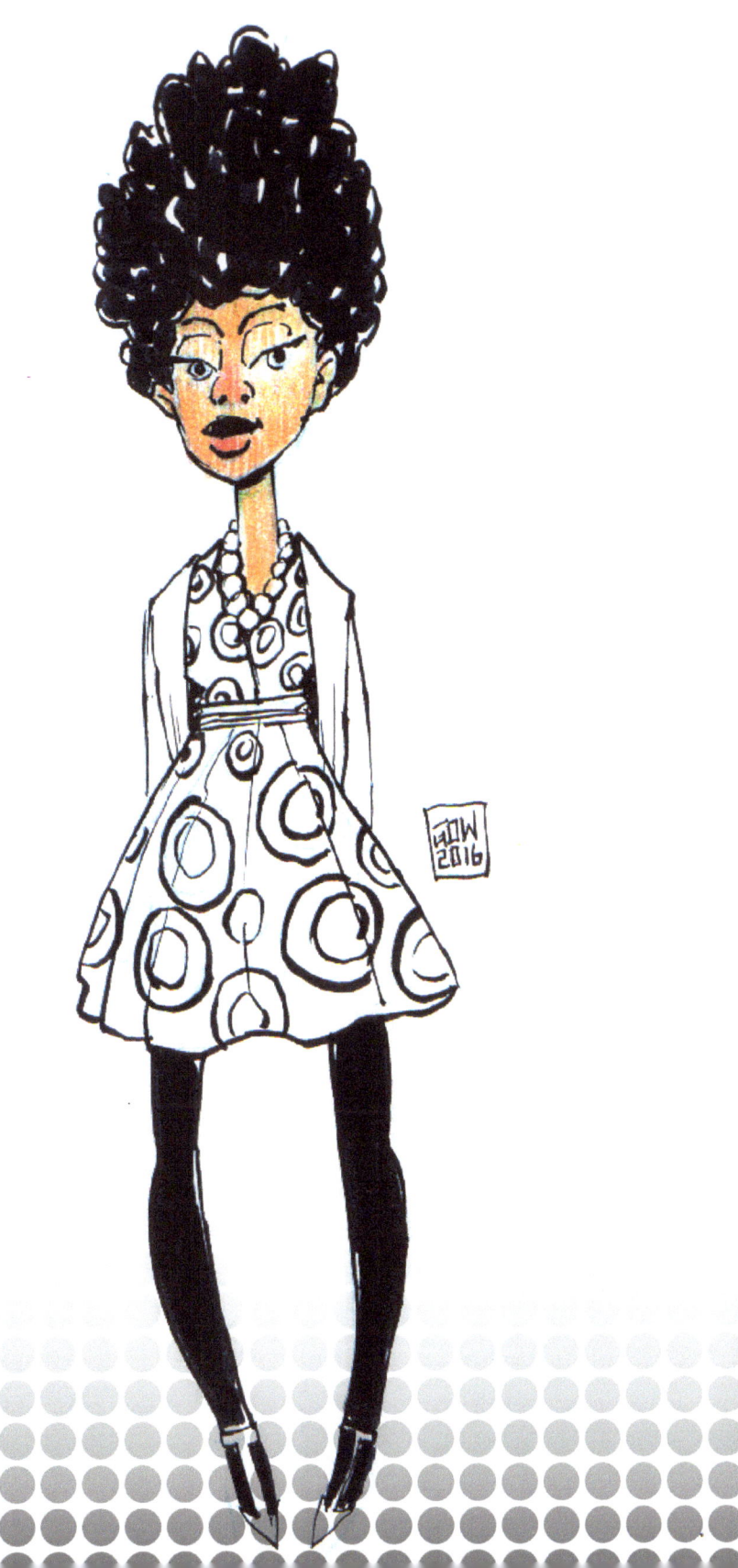

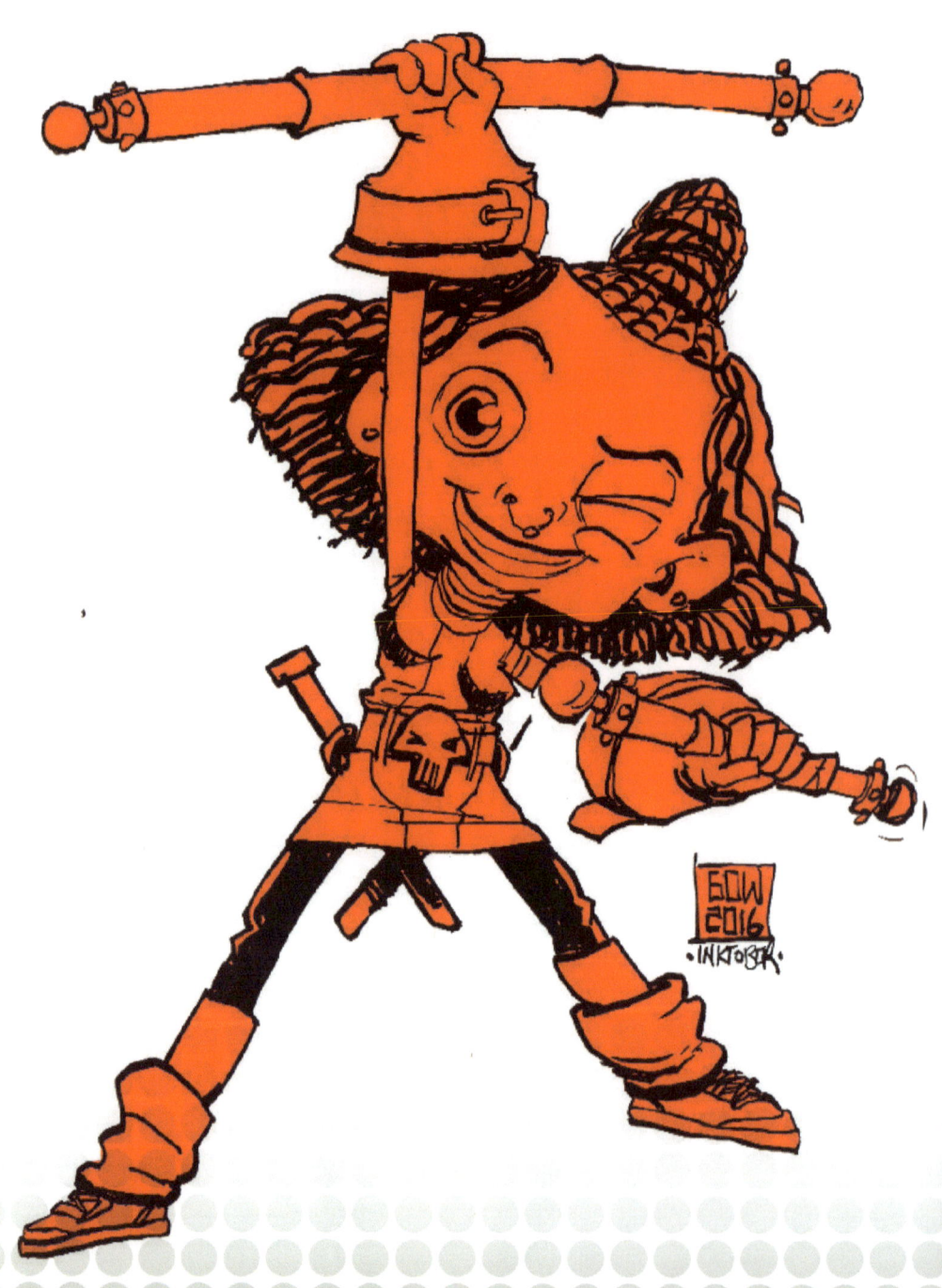

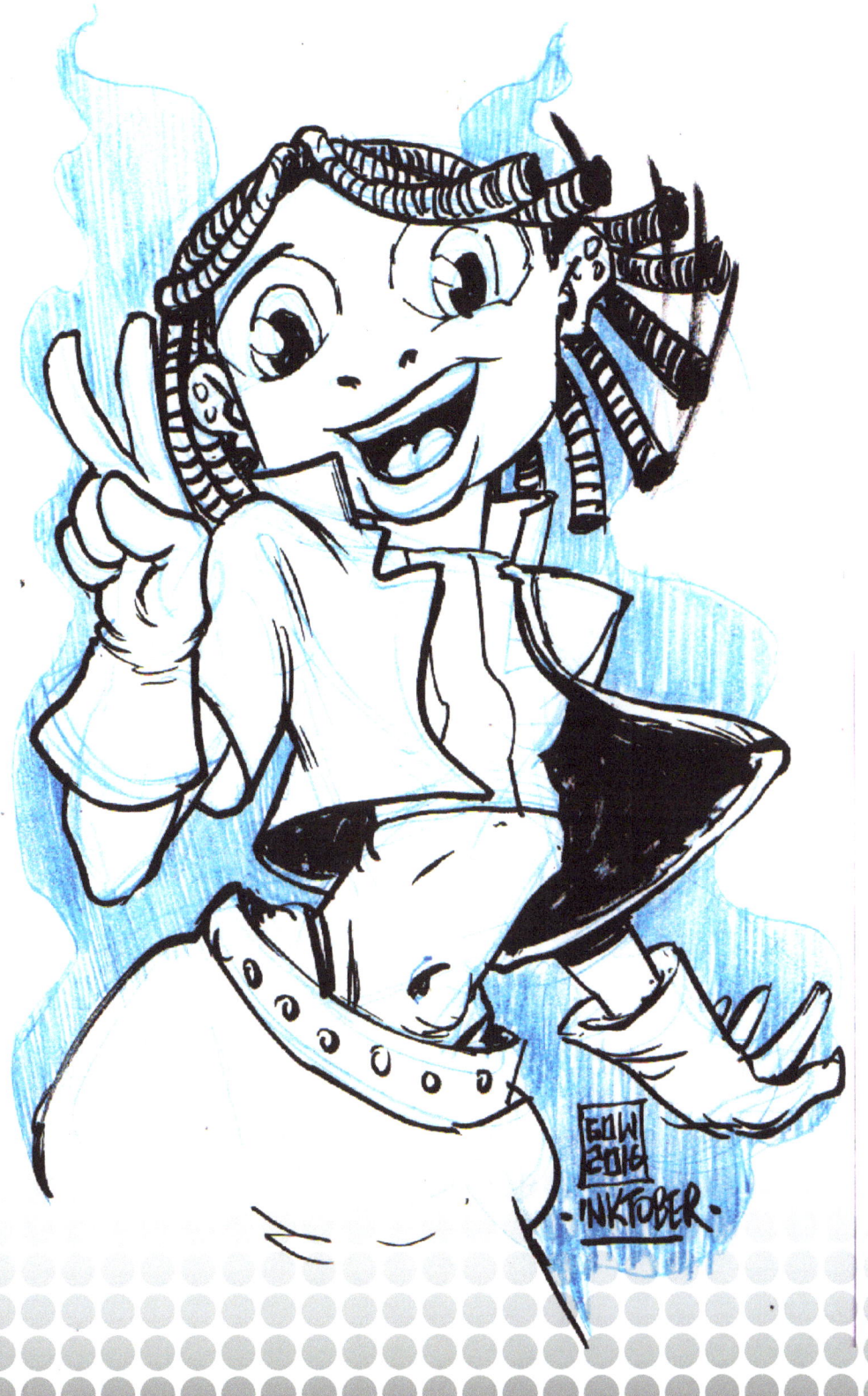

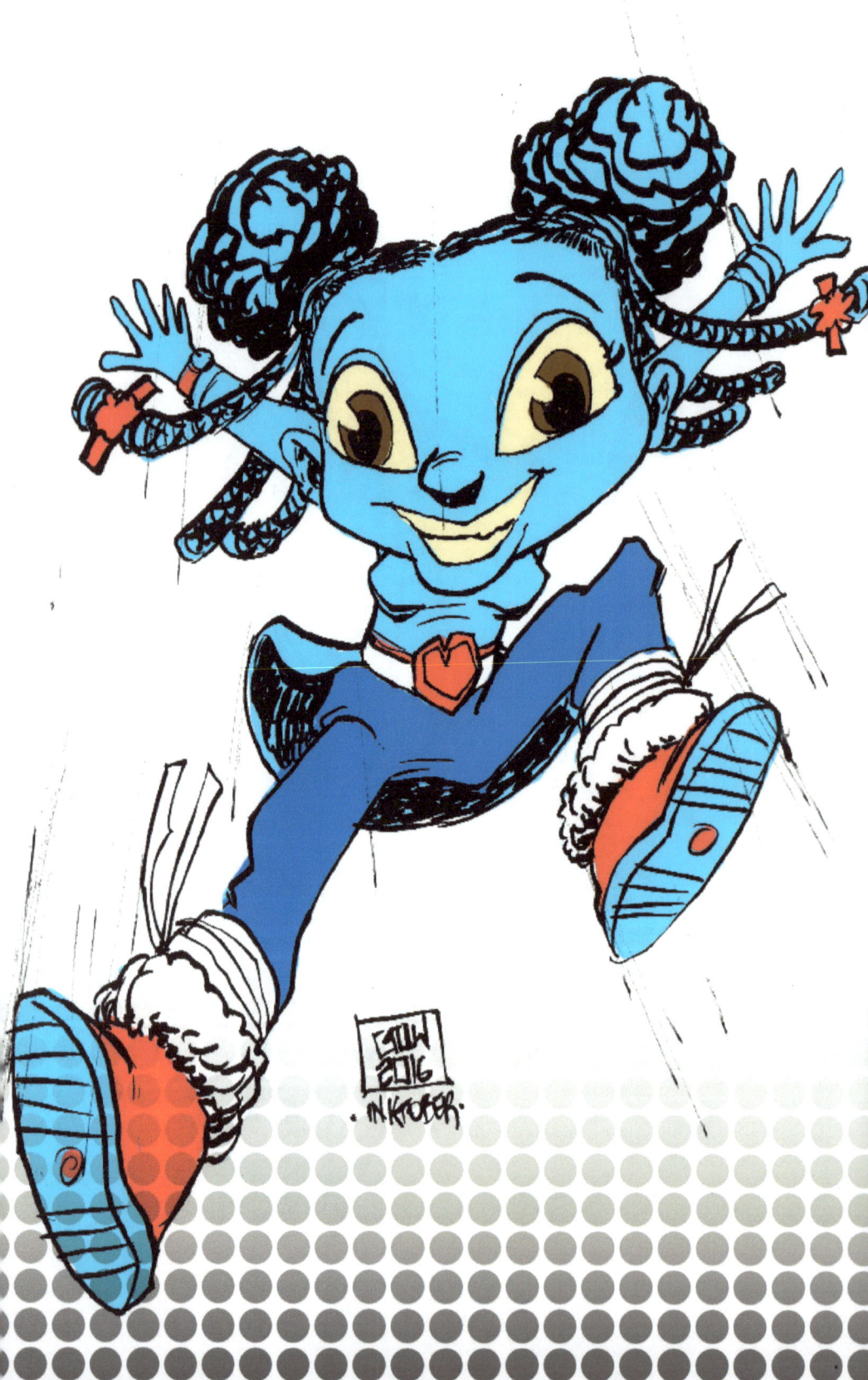

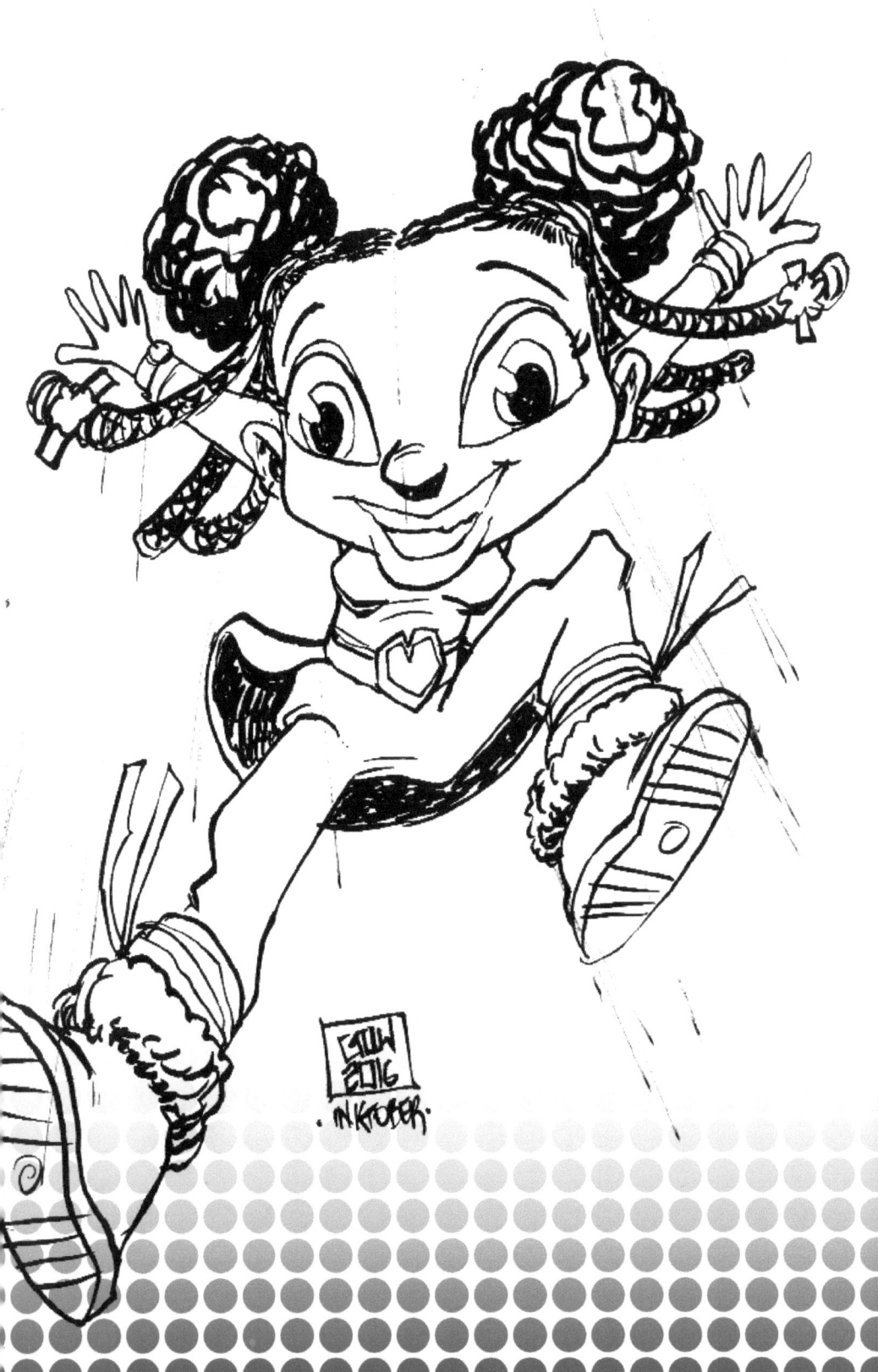

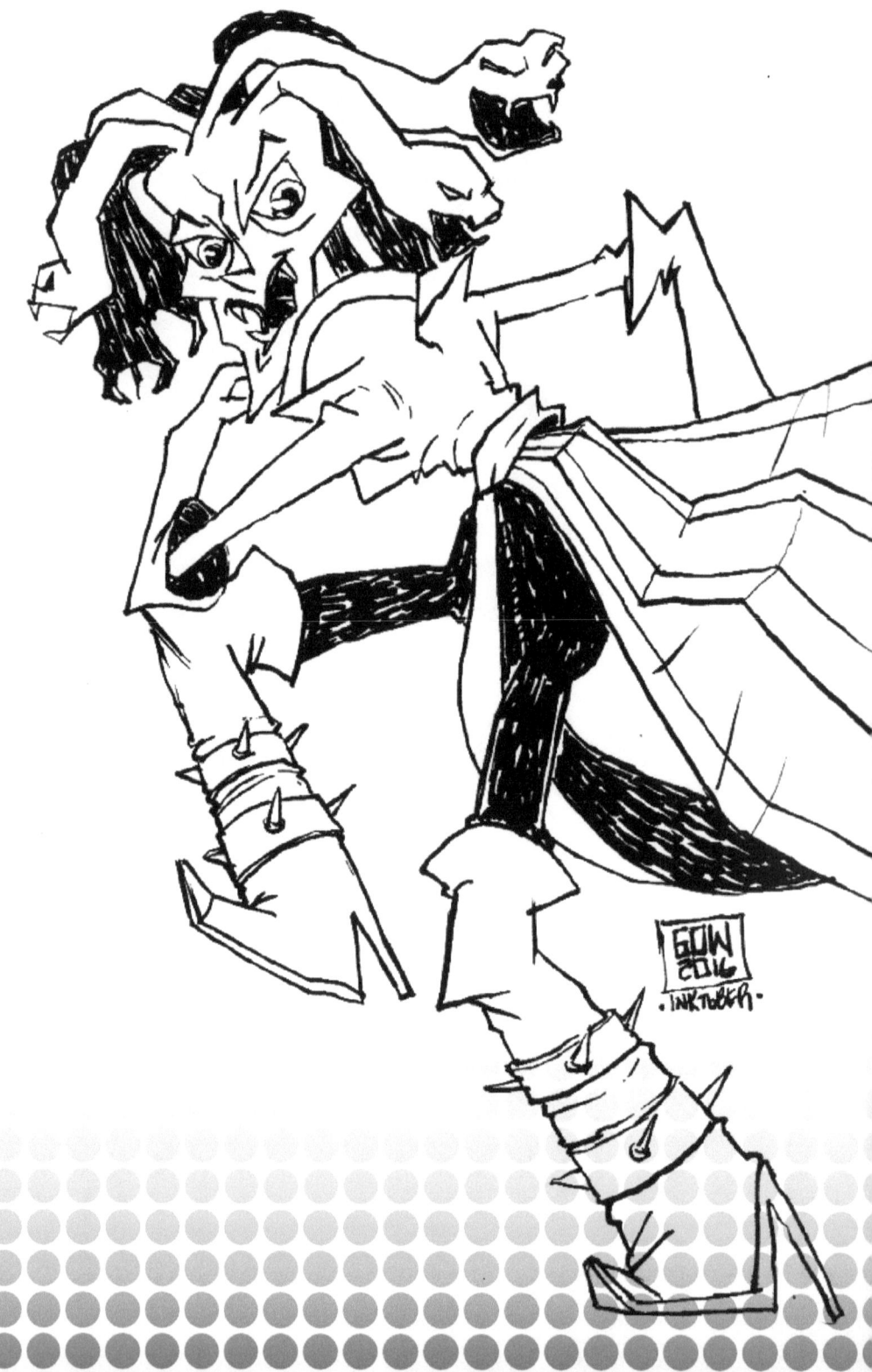

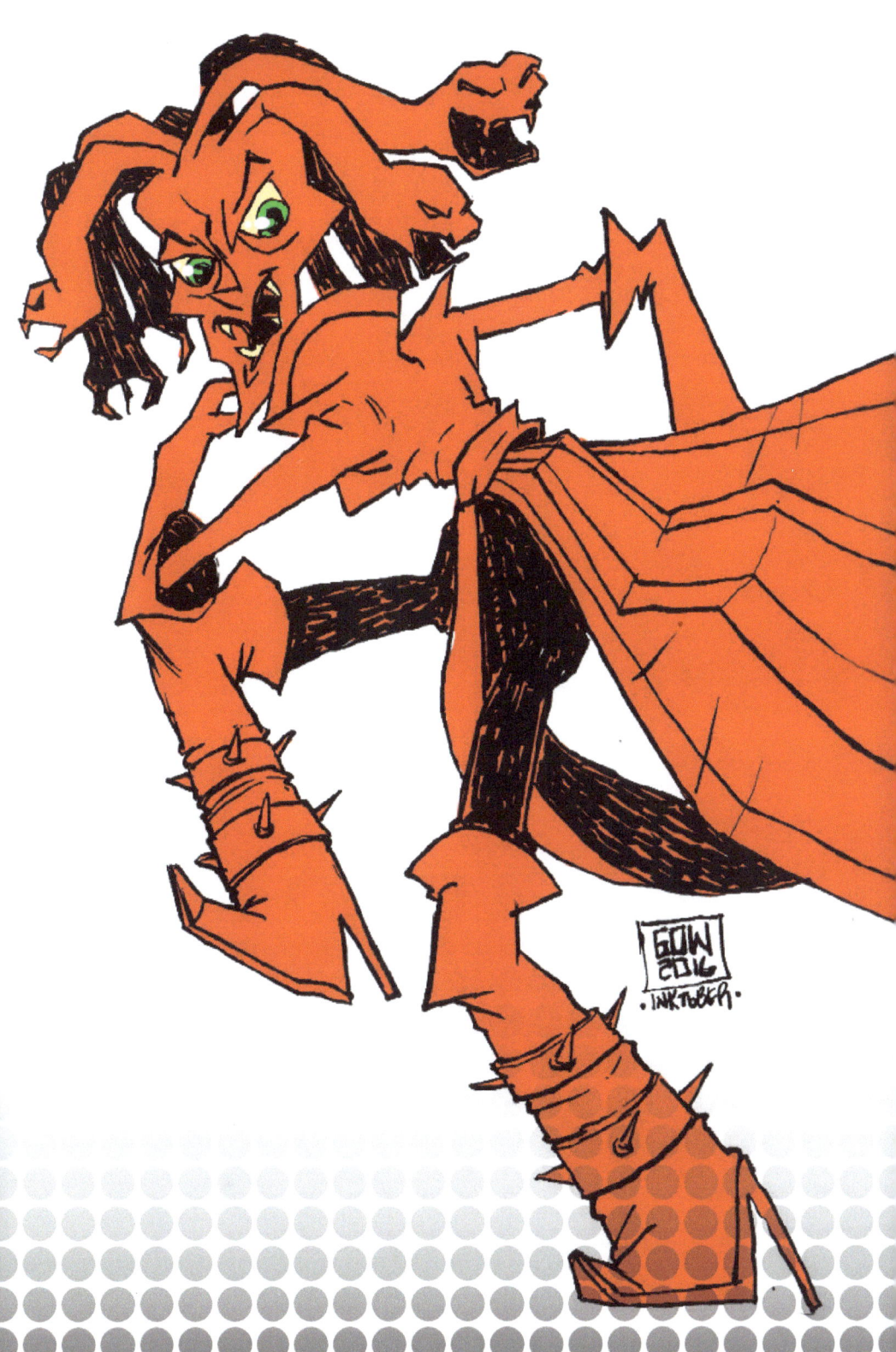

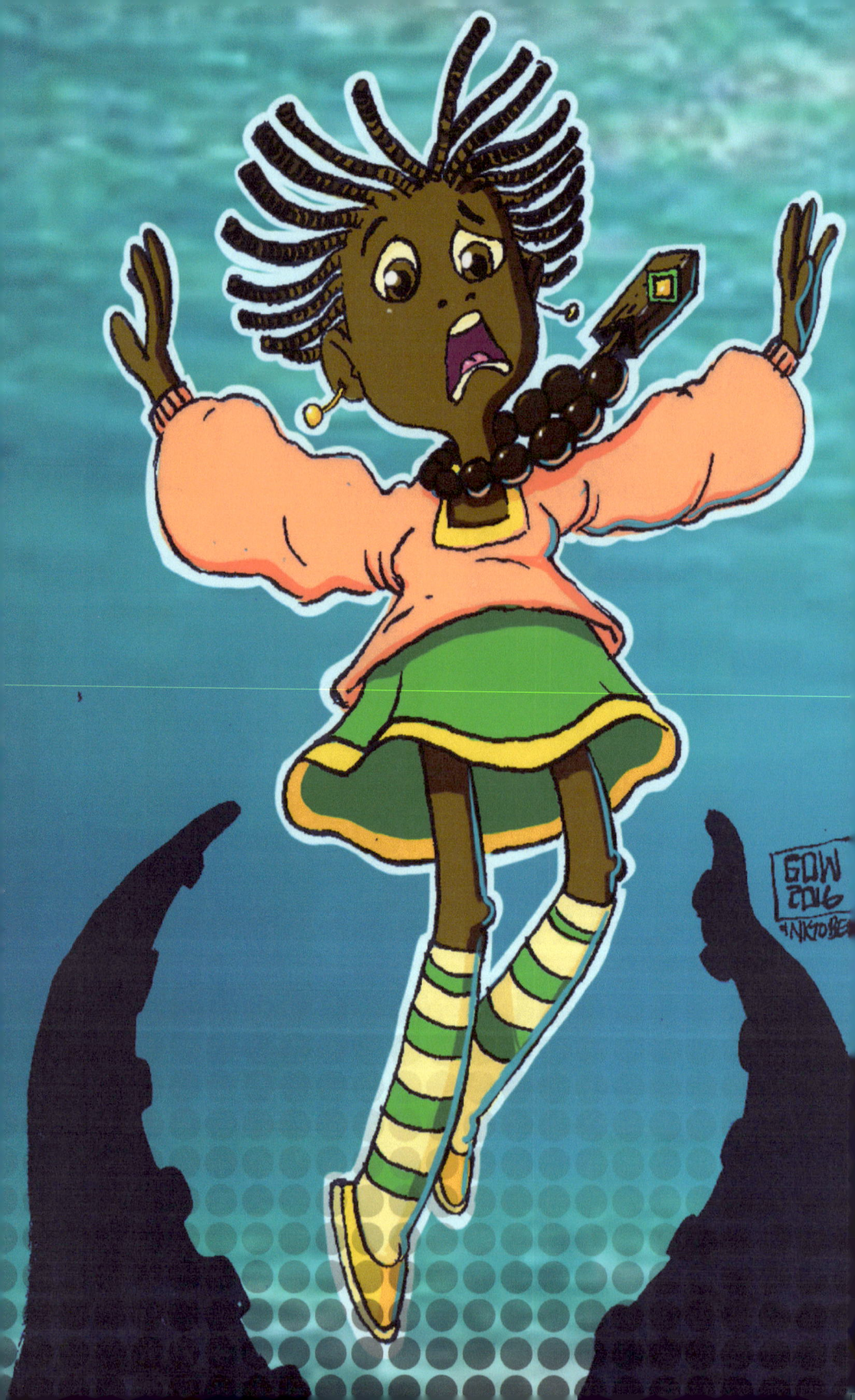

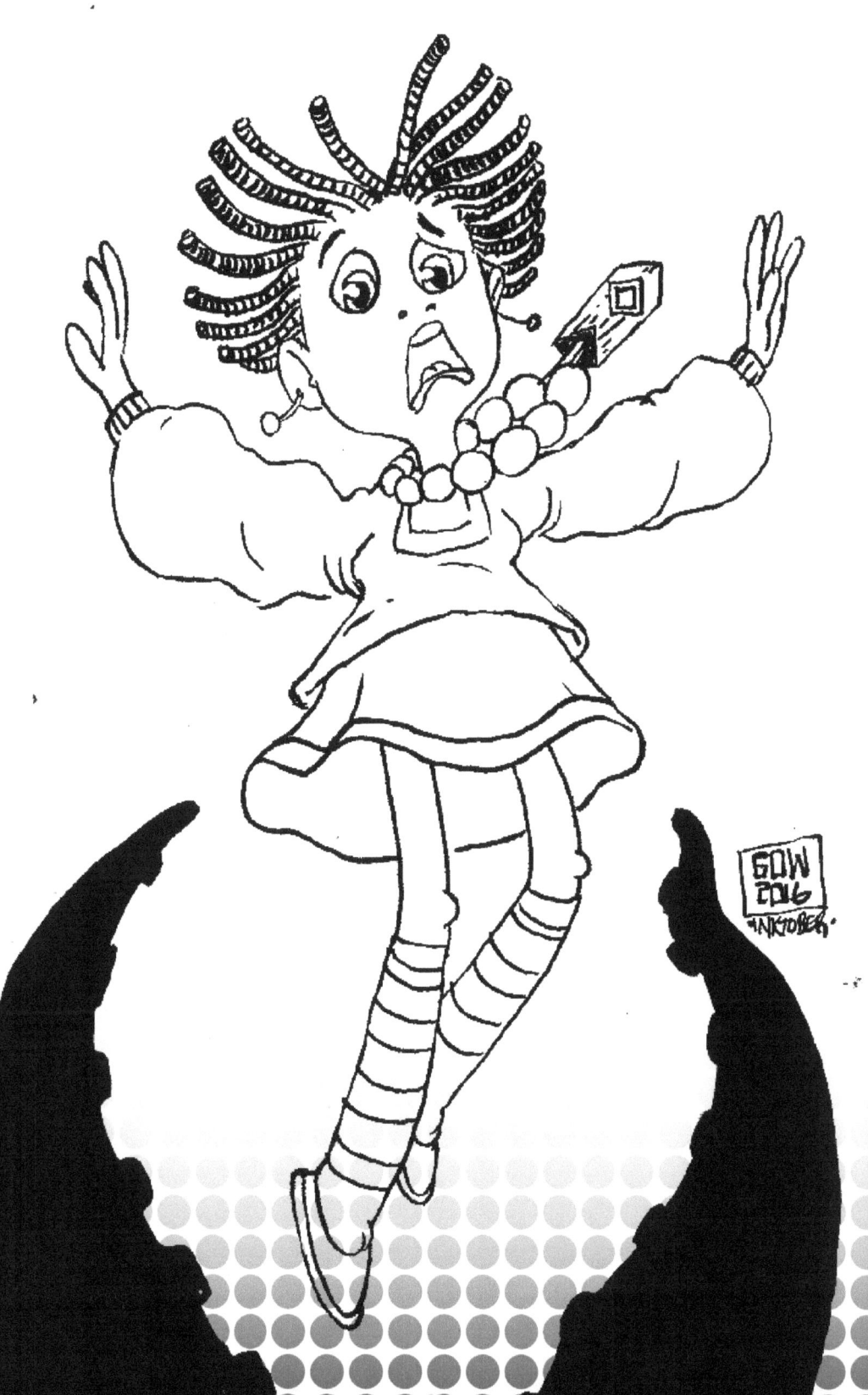

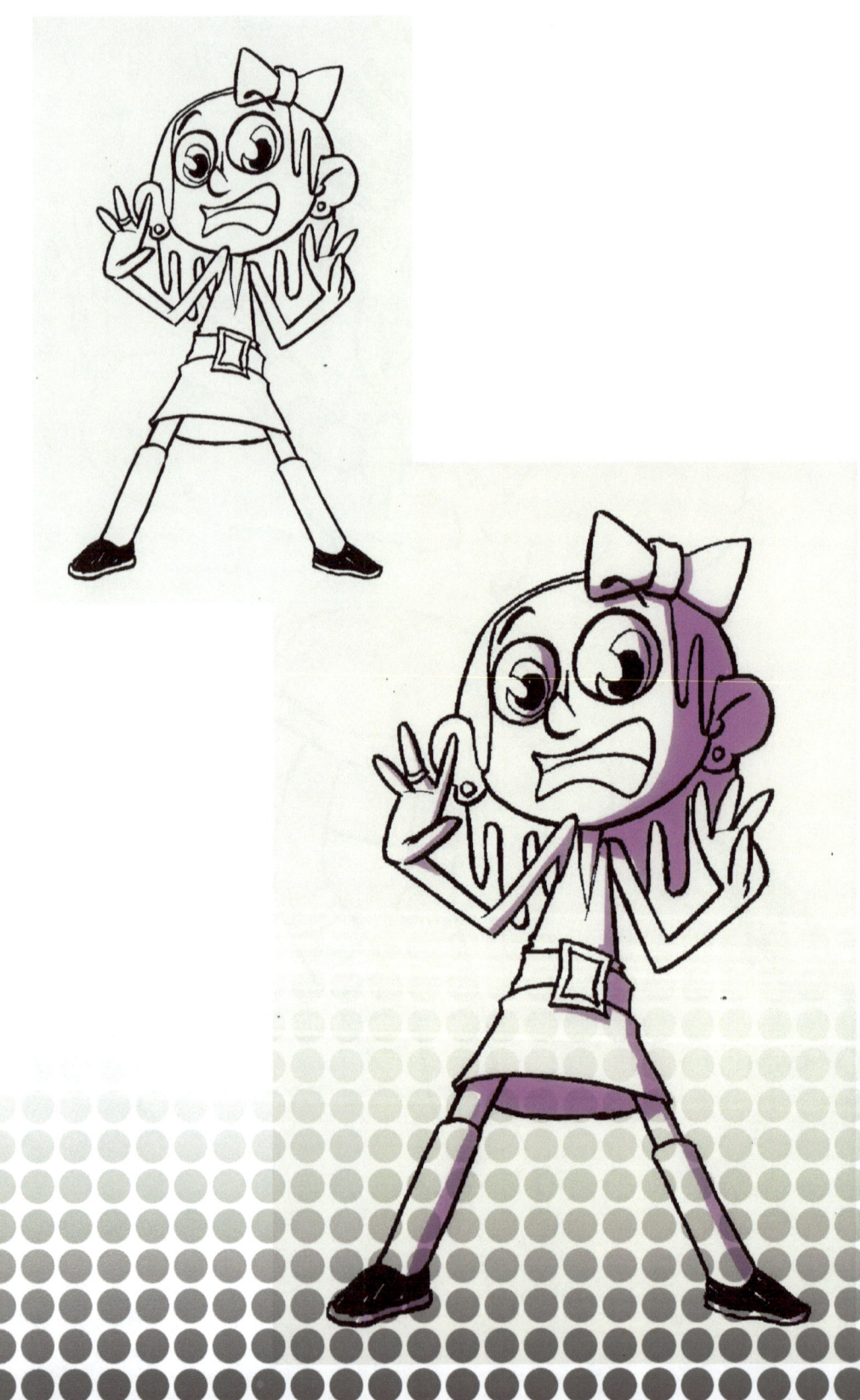

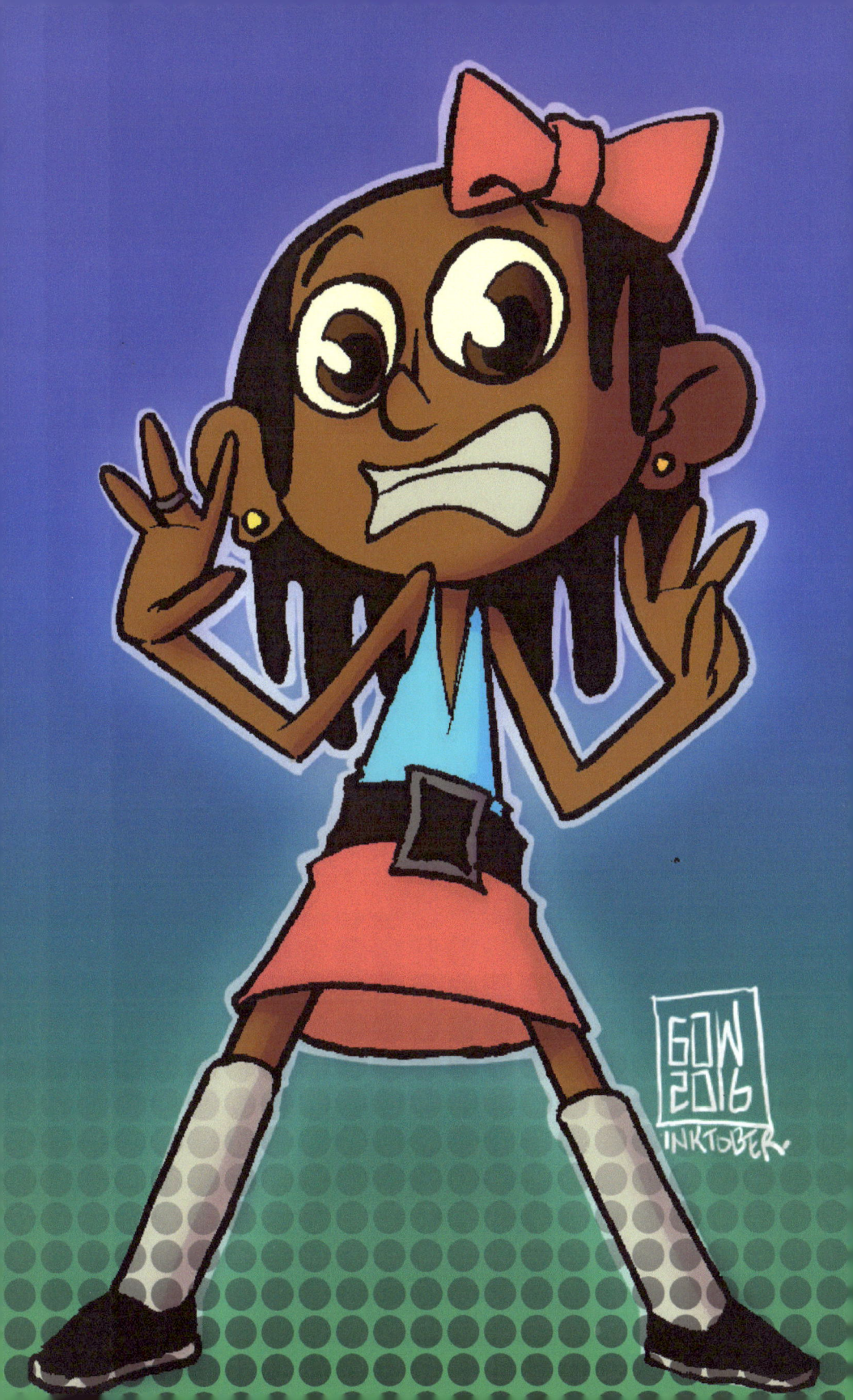

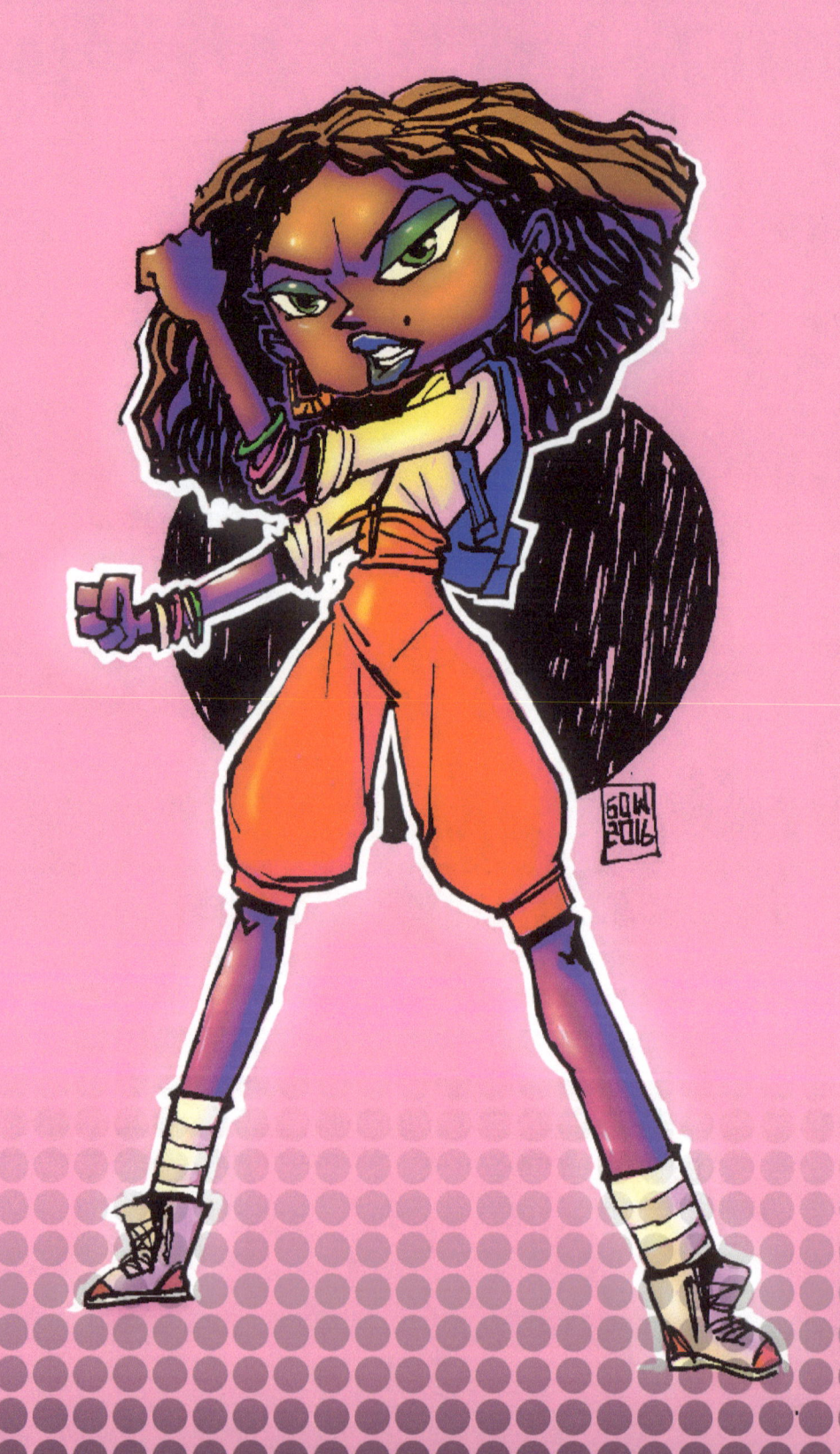

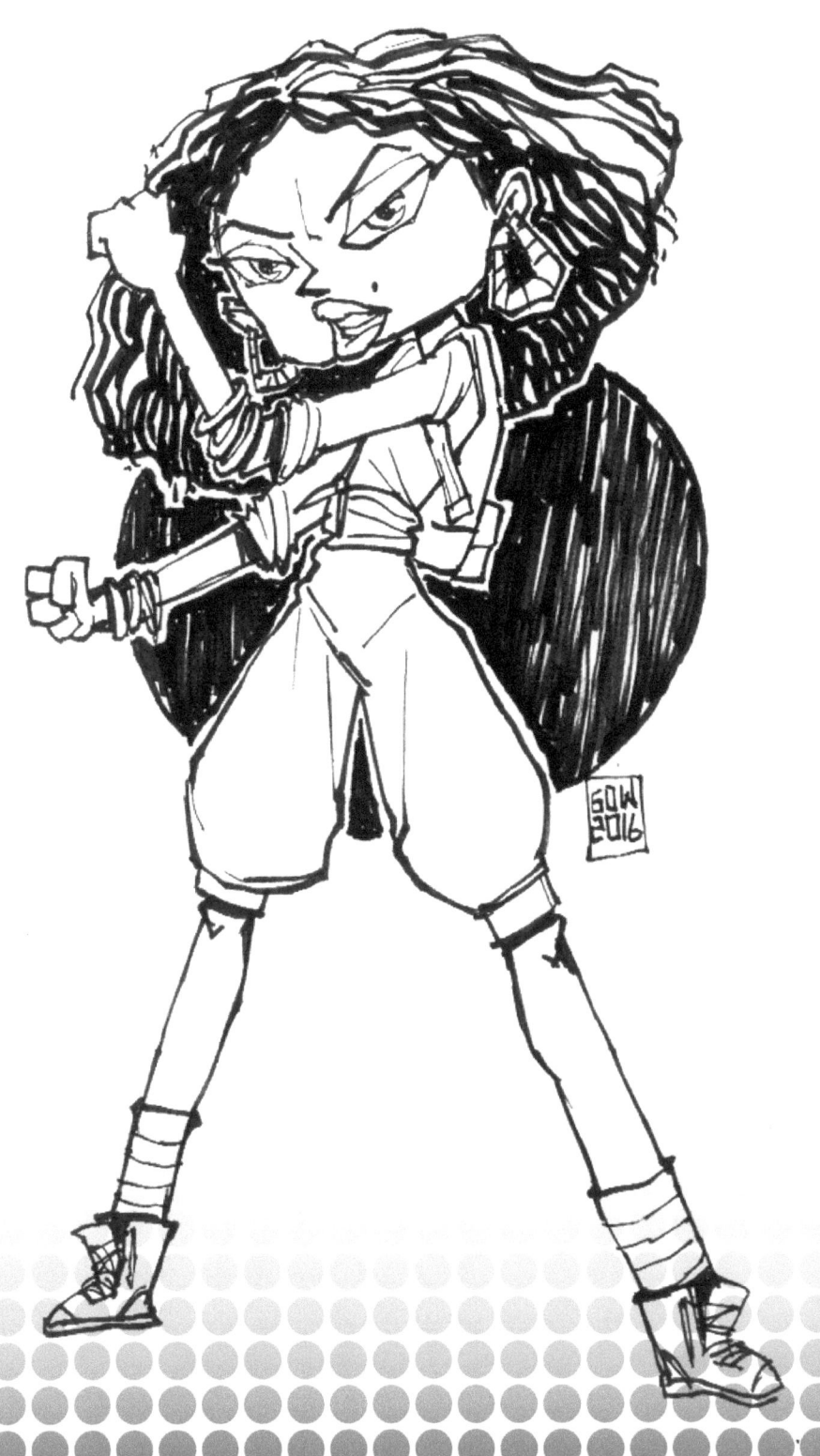

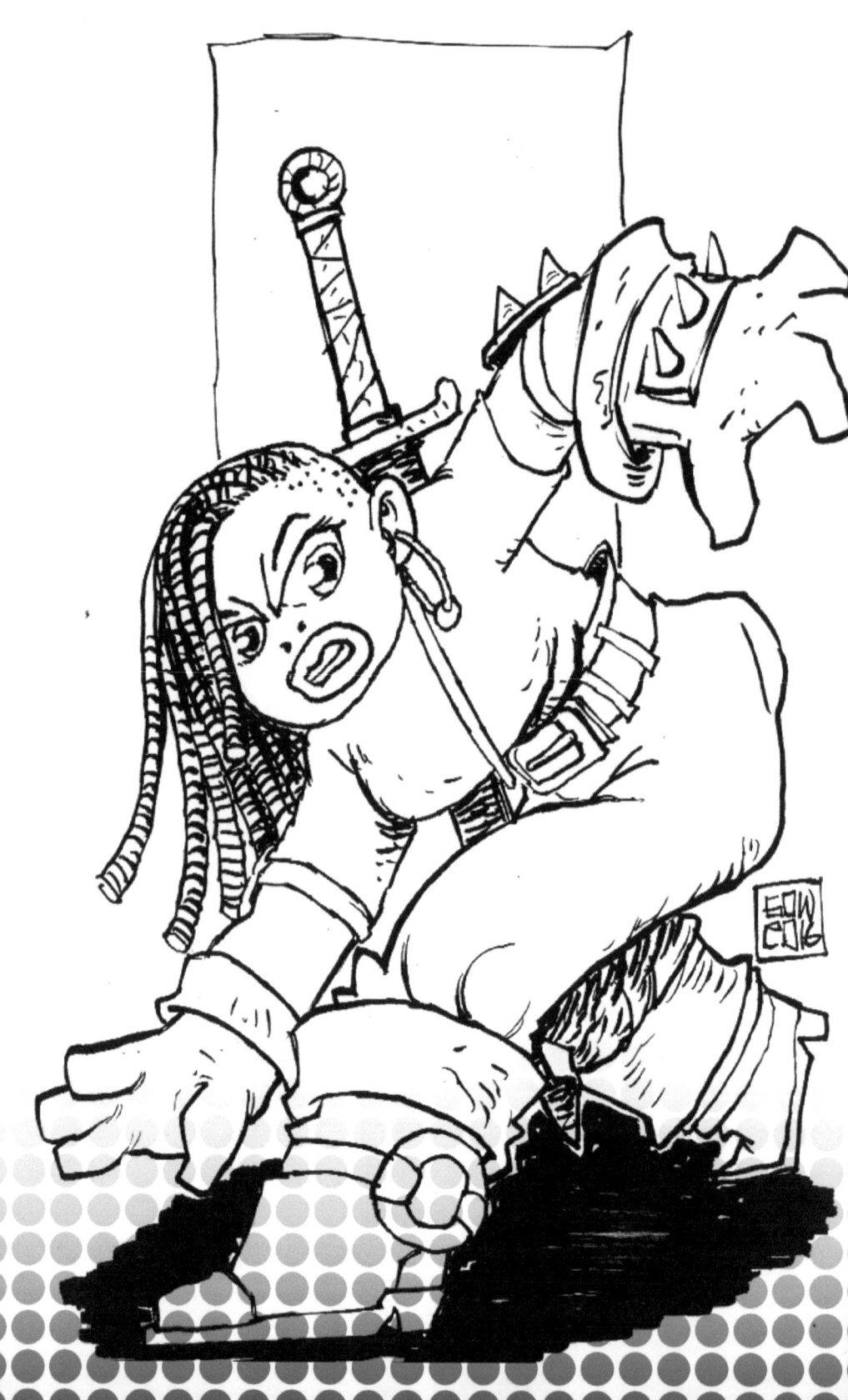

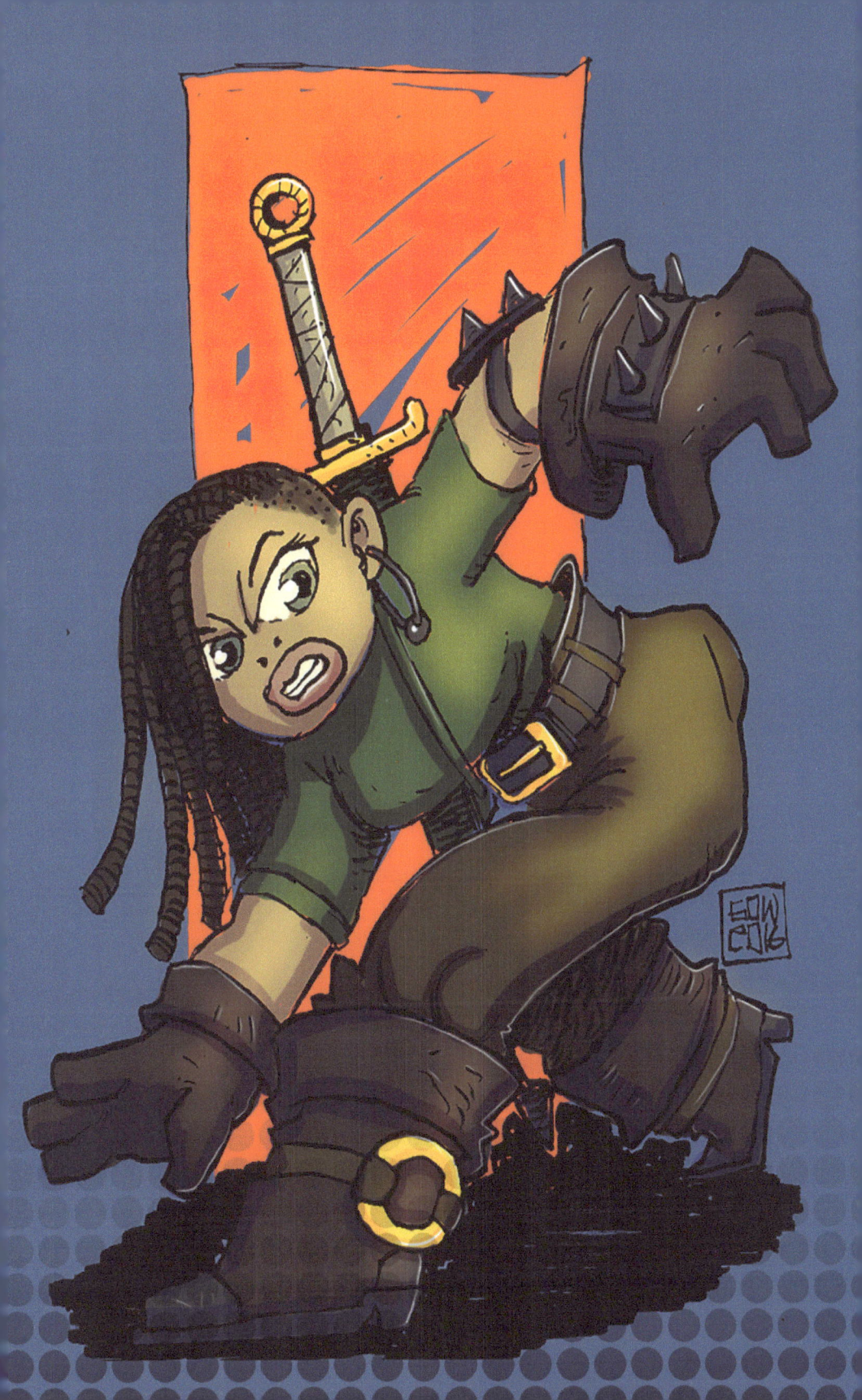

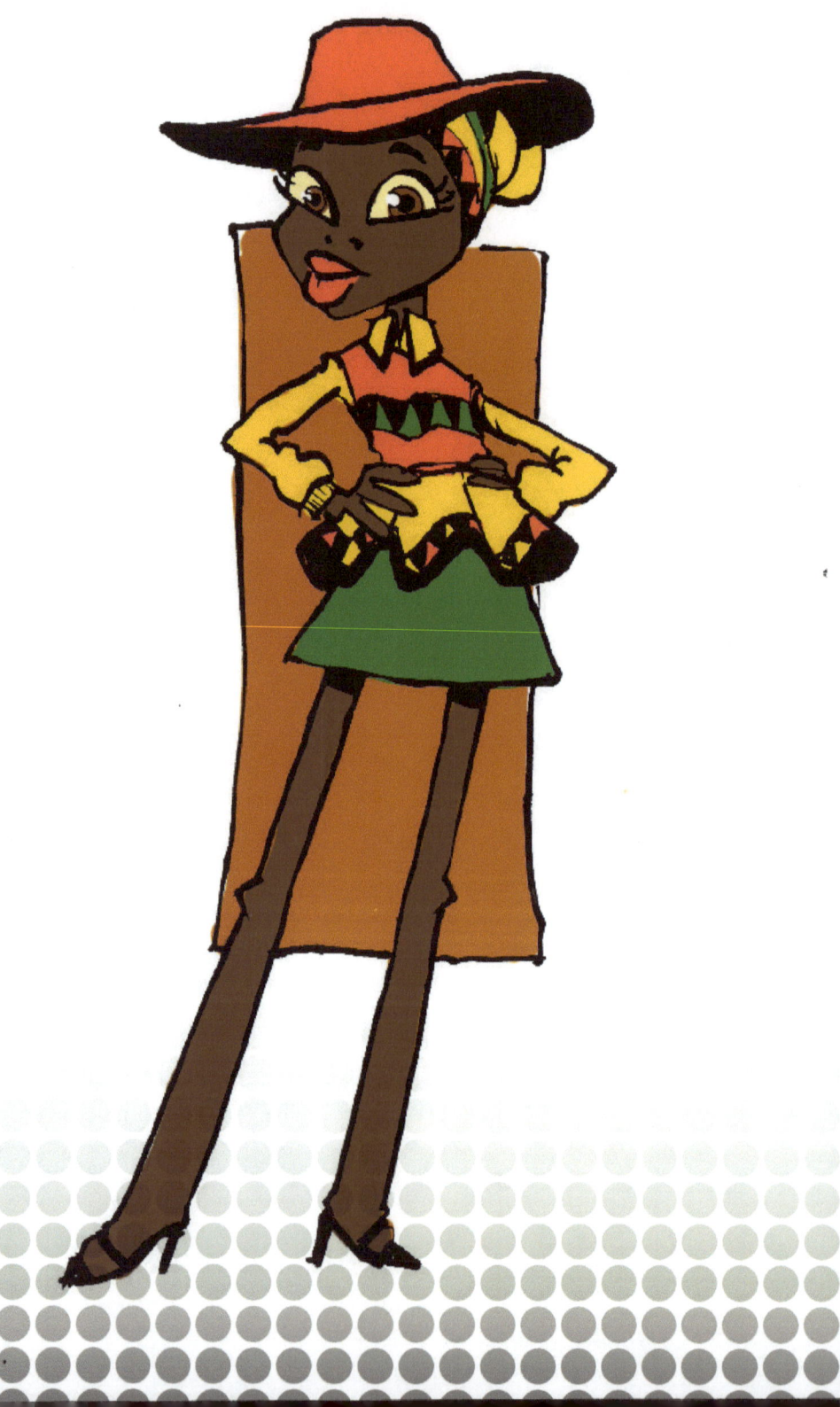

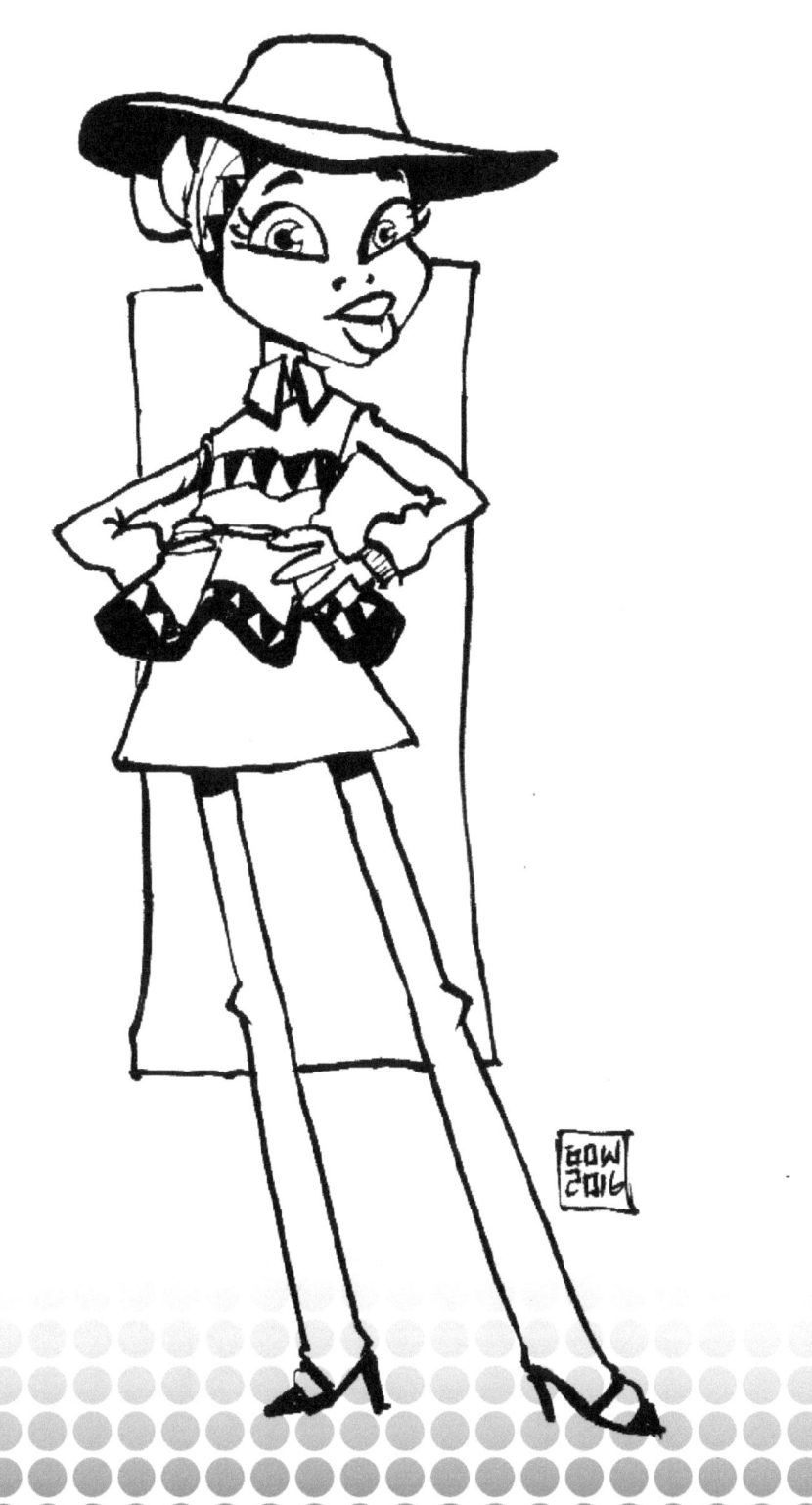

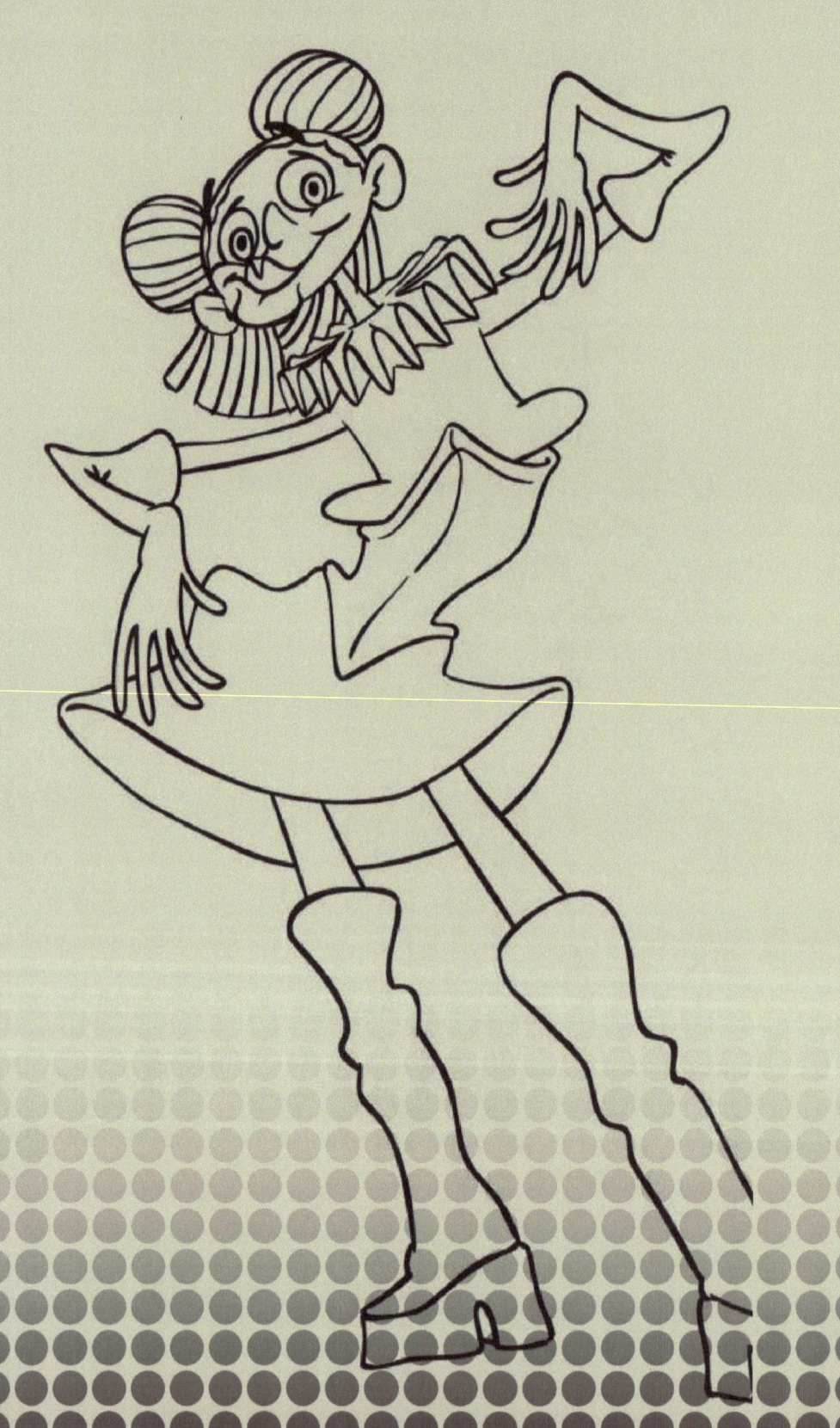

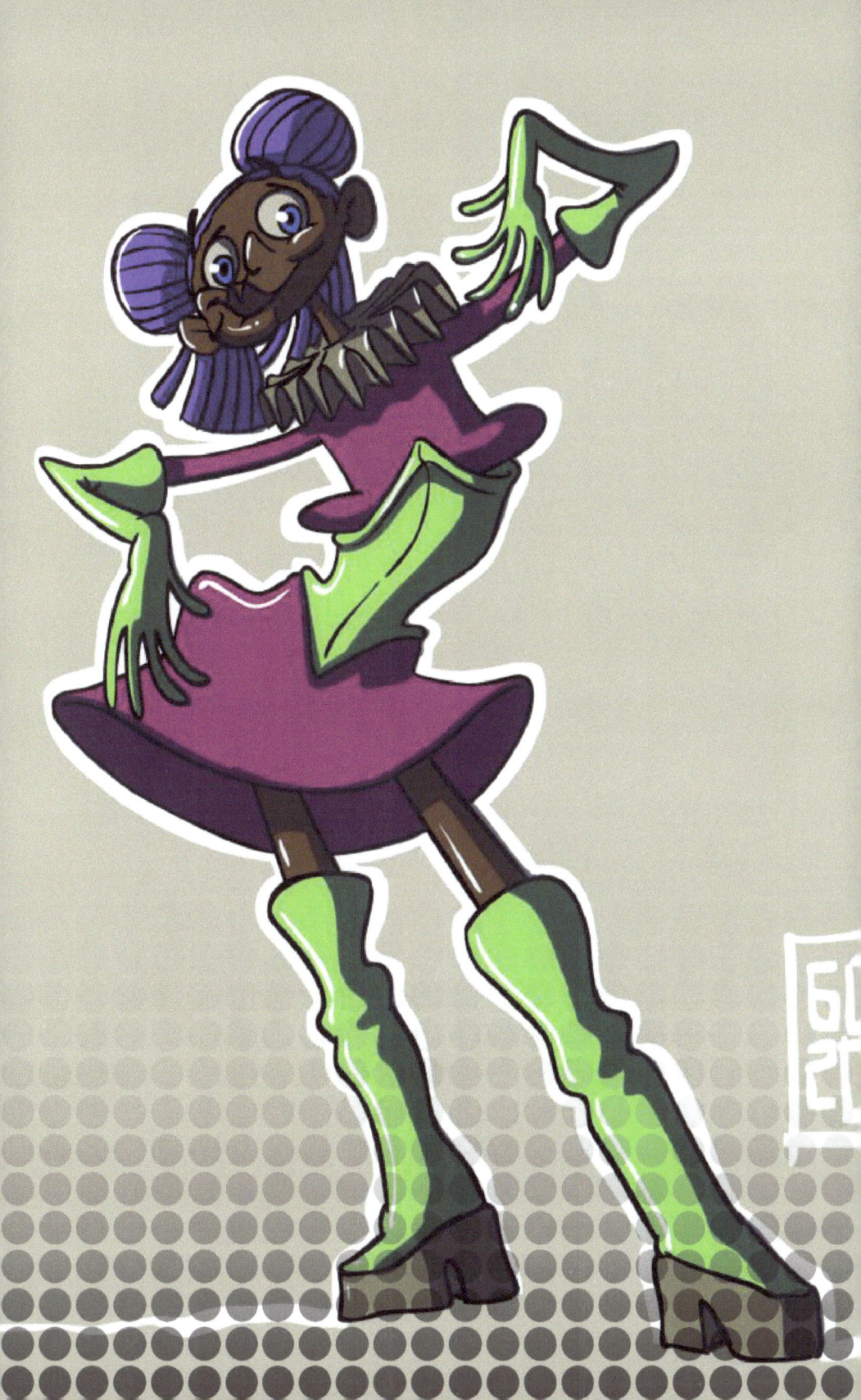

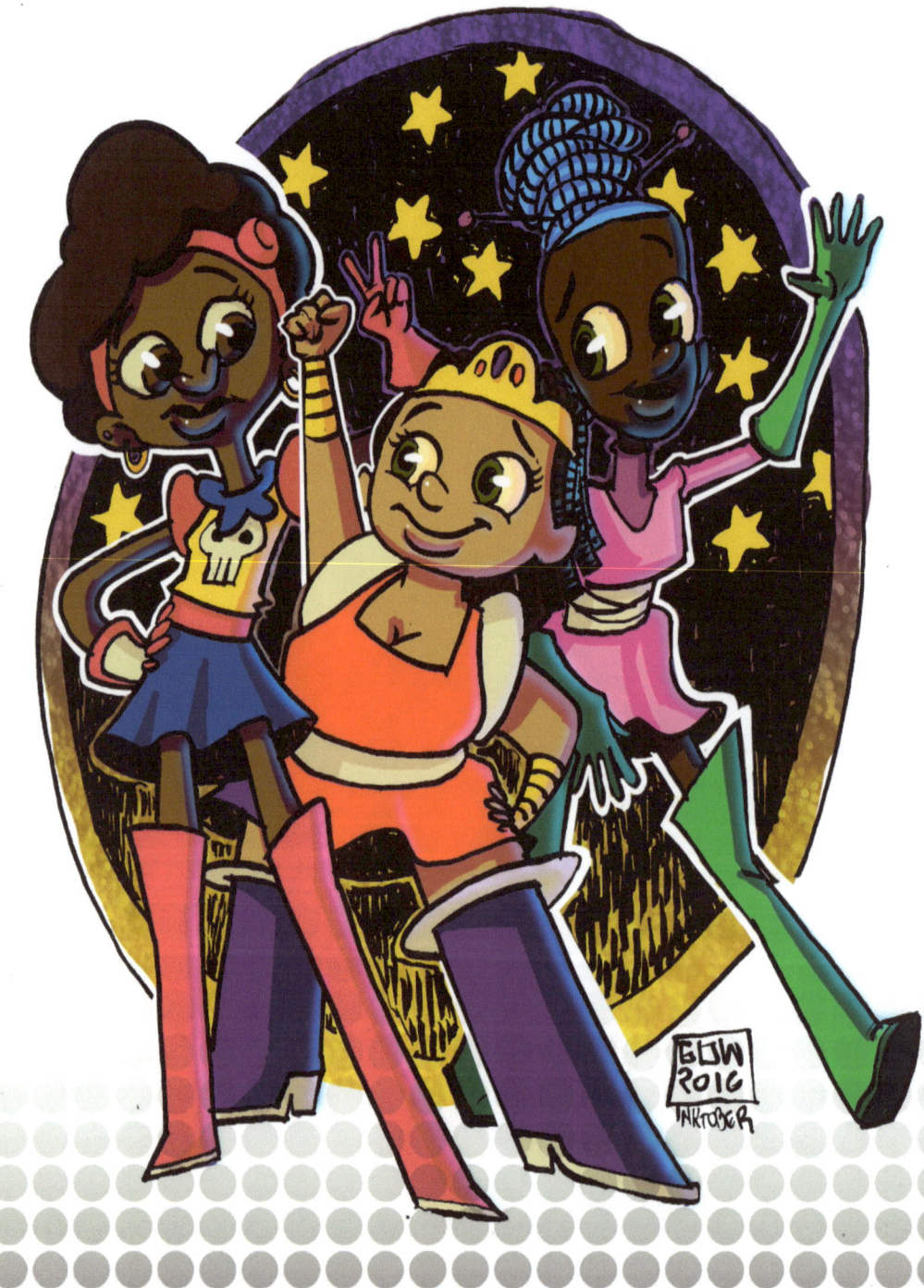

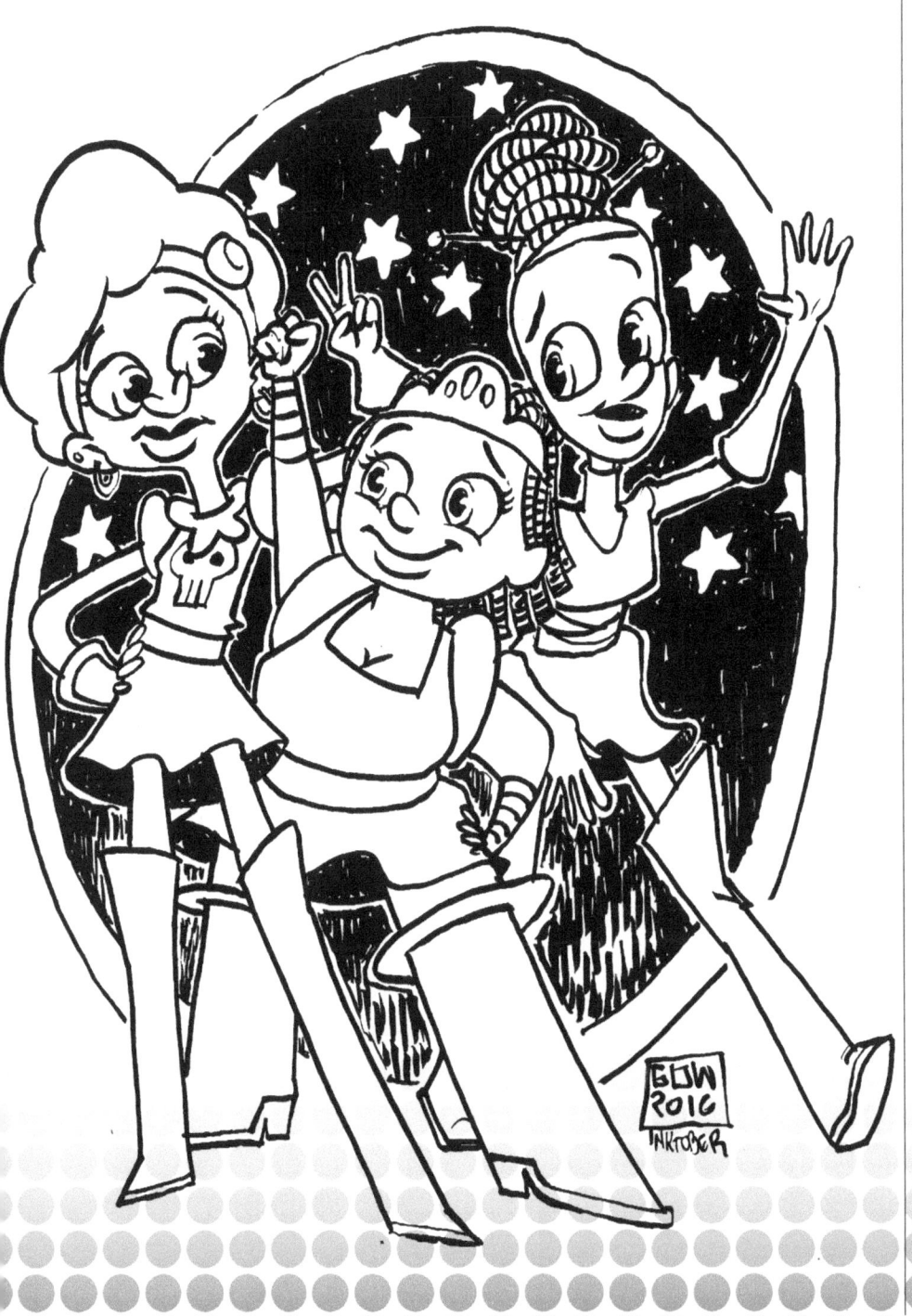

Thank you for buying this collection of drawings.

Check out my website

WWW.AMUSIN.COM

I greatly appreciate the support
and am available for hire.

contact me:

EMAIL - gw@amusin.com
TWITTER - @gradeafun
INSTAGRAM - @gradeafun
YOUTUBE - YOUTUBE.COM/GRADEAFUN
FACEBOOK - GRADEAFUN